How Did This Happen?

By

Victoria & Niamh Salter

Copyright © 2023 by – Victoria Salter – All Rights Reserved.

It is not legal to reproduce, duplicate, or transmit any part of this document in either electronic means or printed format. Recording of this publication is strictly prohibited.

Table of Contents

Dedication i
Acknowledgments ii
About the Author iii
Leap Year 2020 1
OUR JOURNEY STARTS 3
INDUCTION 10
CONSOLIDATION 37
INTERIM MAINTENANCE 46
DELAYED INTENSIFICATION 58
LONG-TERM MAINTENANCE 72
Epilogue 120

Dedication

This book is dedicated to my phenomenal family.

Acknowledgments

To all the amazing people we met on our journey. You and your children are truly astounding. You are all stronger than you will ever know.

The staff that support you on this journey are a constant. It is a dedication to work in this field of medicine and you were all meant for this purpose.

To the families who may read this book, firstly I am so sorry if this journey is part of your lives, I sincerely hope reading this helps you in some small way.

About the Author

Victoria is mum to 2 girls Issy & Niamh. She is married to Kevin a police officer, they were childhood sweethearts and have been together for 25 years! Victoria is a nurse who has worked her whole career mainly in the Accident & Emergency department, recently moving to a GP practice to be able to have a better work/life balance and enjoy weekends with her precious family. Niamh is an extremely head strong 9 year old. She was our inspiration when going through her gruelling treatment.

Leap Year 2020

Life is busy, isn't it? Busy and great. We are just a typical family, both working parents in shift jobs. Lots of hobbies for girls and always on the go!

I am Victoria a nurse practitioner. I have worked in A&E for 15 years and Urgent Care as a practitioner for the past 2 years. Kevin is a police inspector working at present in charge of a response team but has previously worked in the control room. His favourite place to work was traffic and armed response where he spent some time, as his claim to fame, recording police interceptors! Issy, 13 is in secondary school, works hard and plays hard. She has lots of different friendship groups and does cheerleading which she loves 4 times a week totalling 12 hours - when preparing for comps, sometimes more! Niamh is 6, baby of the family, she is very popular with her school friends and follows in her big sister's footsteps also loving cheerleading, and there nearly as much as Issy! Neither of them geniuses, very middle of the road academically, but both very sociable girls.

A typical week would find Kev and I like ships in the night often passing each other between different shift patterns in order for us to be there individually for the girls. Both workaholics in some ways, with demanding and fulfilling jobs. We both enjoy our work, thankfully, as it is a big part of our lives. Both of us are proud to say we have never had a day off sick…this was to dramatically change! The girls appreciate our work and understand we work hard to have our best life with lots of holidays. Although that being said, Issy when she was younger, and Niamh now, both hate me going onto a night shift!

This is where Grandma and Gramps come in. My mum and stepdad live close by, and the girls treat their house like a second home. So much so they have their own bedrooms decorated there! Grandad (Kev's dad) is always on hand to babysit overlapping shifts at ours and lifts to and from cheer. Although 77 he still works driving buses

5 days a week! Papa and Nanny (my dad and stepmum) live in Spain and we try to visit them every school holidays, sometimes with them flying over to pick girls up and have them in Spain whilst Kev and I work.

We are very lucky to have great families although spread far and wide. Kev has a brother in Wales and sister in Fort William, we are very close to them and their children and meet up whenever we can. My brother works abroad, and his girlfriend is from Thailand so we don't see them much. We both have aunties, uncles and cousins with whom we are all very close.

Friends, where do I start! We both have the most amazing friends ever. Many different groups of friends between us all. Firstly, my work friends as I call them although many I don't work with anymore. We may not see each other for months on end but a night out is always one to remember! Also, the girls' weekend holiday we try to get once a year, I'm sure I could write a whole book on stories from them which may be a lot more entertaining than this read! Niamh's godparents Mel and Andrew will feature heavily throughout this book and their help was invaluable. Kev's work friends again very much like mine, we may have met through work, but the friendship continues much longer than working in the same department does! Kev's school friends still all live close by and have kids around the same age as ours, whereas my 2 best friends from school have both moved away, although when seeing each other maybe once a year or even longer, feels like I saw them yesterday! Then there's the cheer mums, school mums, neighbours and many more friends.

OUR JOURNEY STARTS

29/2/2020

Issy and Niamh competed in a large cheerleading competition both receiving 1st prizes and Issy getting highest marks with her stunt team in the whole competition. I was on a hen do as hadn't realised it was the same week as the competition, so Ruby (one of the girls' friend's) mum, Allison, took them, as Kev was working. Niamh was so very well. She had bloods done by the GP 3 weeks previously to this as she kept getting non-blanching rashes on various parts of her body. The day after we had her bloods done, we were told to go to hospital as they had concerns about her low platelets. This was no real surprise to me as I was concerned she had idiopathic thrombocytopenia or ITP as she was regularly getting these rashes. ITP is a type of platelet disorder it means your blood does not clot due to having a low platelet count. However, on the paediatric ward at our local hospital we were reassured it was not this nor was it anything to be concerned about, we were told, 'It was viral'. I was surprised they diagnosed it as viral as she had not been unwell at all. Anyway, they wanted to repeat bloods in 2 weeks and reassured us they expected them to improve. We had a lovely four days in Spain, over February half term, staying with my dad and stepmum. Niamh got a rash whilst we were away, but it went very quickly, and she was as fighting fit as always! We returned on the day she needed her bloods, went to hospital where they struggled to get them trying five times which upset her. It was a long day as I then went and did a nightshift. I rang for Niamh's results the next day and struggled to get anyone to tell me them. Finally, I spoke to a nurse practitioner who informed me the levels had all reduced again. Now I started to worry!

I rang the consultant we had seen on the ward, however, was unable to get in touch, I rang his secretary again- no luck and didn't actually hear from another consultant until four days later. He asked how Niamh was. I told him honestly, I thought she was fine - going to school and doing cheerleading however, I now had concerns. He reassured me her bloods were not concerning and they would repeat them again in two weeks.

This leads me to the day after the cheer competition.

2/3/2020 DAY 0

Niamh went to school, after work I came home and collected her from her friends as she had walked home with her, and her mum. She told me off for picking her up too early as she hadn't had time to play! We then came home and had tea with Issy. Kev was at work. She was sat on the sofa watching TV and she called me in- she was upset and said she had a tummy ache. I said she was probably tired, and I would give her a bath. When I put her in the bath, I noticed her stomach was protruding and had completely swelled up. Issy came in to see her and said she looked like, 'One of those malnutrition children you see on TV'. I rung my friend at work and said I think I'll have to bring Niamh over and explained why. They said come straight away knowing it is not like me to be overly concerned. On seeing Niamh, they were also extremely worried, the practitioner rung the paediatric team to explain Niamh had been having tests under their care. However, they said she now sounded too poorly for them to see, and we were transferred to Accident and Emergency. We were seen there by an amazing registrar who even scanned her abdomen. He gave us many differential diagnoses however, said that his thoughts were leukaemia! In the back of my mind, I think I thought that he could still be wrong! It was only the last couple of hours she had felt unwell - surely, she couldn't have leukaemia? We were transferred to the children's ward and after getting Niamh settled, I nipped home as I was still in my works outfit and got us some bits. When I returned Kev was in a room with the paediatric consultant and two other Drs, realisation kicked in …. They were, as we call it in the business, 'breaking bad news'. Niamh's bloods had not come back however, they had spoken to the 'Great North Children's Hospital' at Newcastle, and they wanted Niamh to be seen there. She was to be transferred first thing in the morning. There was still hope, I thought. They could all still be wrong! Had they not been reassuring us for the past four weeks that she was fine? Niamh and I settled down in our hospital room and Kev went home. People came in and out all night. Niamh's bloods were lost! Another Dr had to retake them. Her levels were dangerously low, and she was started on intravenous antibiotics, potassium and fluid. I was told at 0200hrs on 3.3.2020 that Niamh was going to be transferred by emergency ambulance to Newcastle. The ambulance still hadn't arrived when Kev came back the next morning, so they decided to take the drips down and let us travel ourselves to Newcastle RVI.

3/3/2020 DAY 1

We were put into a cubicle and Niamh was not allowed anything to eat or drink. Another Dr saw Niamh and she put in yet another intravenous cannula and took bloods explaining that the consultant haematologist would look at the blood and be able to give us a diagnosis. The consultant 'Geoff' came to see us and asked to talk to us privately. He told us he was 90% certain it was leukaemia however, there was still a small chance it wasn't, but in order to confirm this, Niamh needed a bone marrow test. Niamh was starved which was good, however, we had to wait for an emergency slot in theatre. We told her she was allowed anything she wanted when she woke from her 'magic sleep' general anaesthetic. She decided she wanted a subway sandwich - very specific chicken, cheese, onion, lettuce and sweet onion sauce with a double chocolate chip cookie!

This I would say was my first point of realisation however, I was still extremely hopeful Niamh would be a phenomenon and she would be in the 10%. Eventually she went into theatre at 1500hrs, she had not eaten since 0600. I went in with her, the theatre staff were amazing very equipped to deal with kids, she was in the 'fairy room' and the anaesthetist told her she was giving her chocolate milkshake. She asked Niamh where she would like to be drinking it, Niamh told her by the pool with her papa in Spain, but it wasn't chocolate it was Oreo as you get that in Spain! She then closed her eyes, and she was sedated. I gave her a kiss and the reality hit like a ton of bricks. I completely broke down.

Kev was waiting for me outside and he wanted me to have something to eat – how could I eat when my baby girl was going through that? We sat on a bench outside the hospital and contemplated what was happening to us, with lots of tears. We were then called back onto another ward where the consultant and specialist leukaemia nurse came to see us. As we walked onto this ward it said, 'Welcome to the Children's Cancer Unit'. I find it hard to put into words how I felt reading that sign! We were taken again into a private room, not quite inside the ward, there we got the devastating news that Niamh had 'ALL' Acute Lymphoblastic Leukaemia. I was numb and heartbroken. Lots of positive words were said 'this is treatable' '90% curable' however, I didn't hear them. This treatment would last over 2 years! At this time this felt a lifetime away....over 2 years! Little did we know what would happen to our world in this time?

This ward was now my reality my beautiful baby had cancer, cancer that was everywhere in her blood. Did I have questions? I had so many where did I start? How would we tell Niamh? What was this treatment going to do to her? How would we tell Issy? How would she cope? So many things to consider but no time, as then we were called to collect Niamh from theatre. I had to compose myself to go into the theatre recovery room, she told us off when we got there, saying we should have been there earlier, as soon as she woke up! She was always able to make me smile! We went onto the ward which would be our home for the next 7 days.

Nothing could have prepared me for that moment when I walked onto that ward. Poorly children, mostly bald from chemotherapy, some with feeding tubes in place, some walking around the ward, others in wheelchairs. This was now Niamh! My little cheerleader with long blonde hair, styled differently everyday by her sister. How did this happen, when she looked so well? We were taken into a private side room with a small pull-down bed for me. The consultant and the specialist nurse came in to see Niamh, they explained to her she had 'naughty blood' and they needed to make it better. My mum, stepdad and Issy came to see Niamh. She got her subway which she had been waiting for. Niamh had seen what I had seen as she was wheeled in a trolley onto the ward, she was subdued and didn't really want to speak to anyone.

When the nurses came and spoke to Niamh and I, to admit her, they explained that everything that comes out of her body needs measuring. So, any urine, faeces or vomit must be kept and the procedure was that I take it to a room called the sluice. Niamh was not up for this and said, 'You are not doing that!' I said, 'I have to!'

When everyone left, I settled Niamh for the night and then the day hit home. I sobbed, for my beautiful daughter who needed to go on this horrendous journey and for the other children on this ward who were already a part of theirs. A doctor came in who said she was consenting Niamh for the next day for theatre…again! This time she would need to have a lumbar puncture (a large needle is inserted into the lower back and a sample of cerebrospinal fluid is taken) and 1st dose of intrathecal chemotherapy (injecting chemotherapy into this fluid). She would also have a portacath (a small device that sits under her skin on her chest) fitted. How quickly was all this happening, I just couldn't get my head around it!

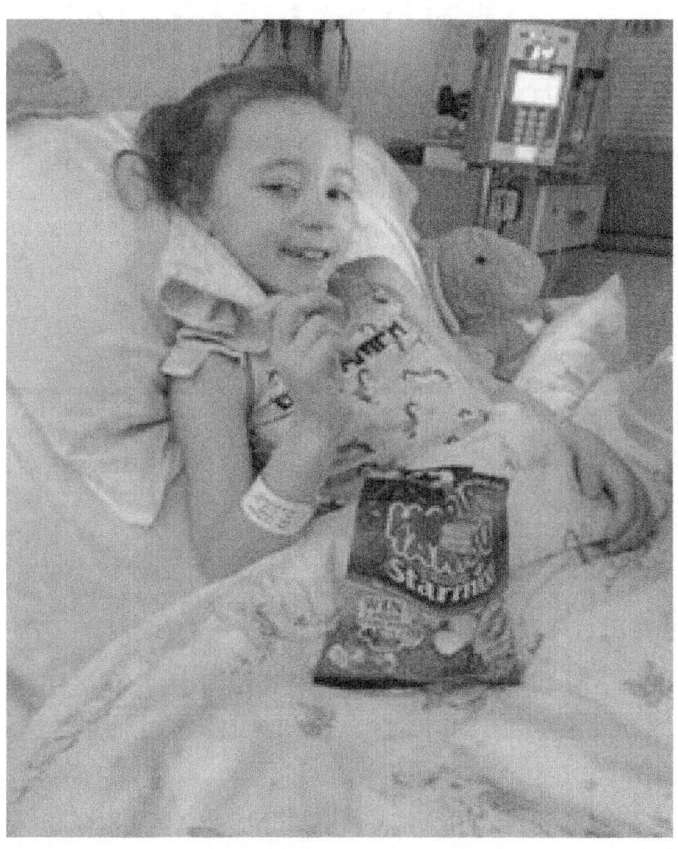

INDUCTION

4/2/2020 DAY 2

Niamh was not able to eat again this morning. In her own words she said to me, 'How can they make me better by starving me?' Again, it was an emergency list so no idea when she would go to theatre. Kev was back early at the hospital, he had brought me some clean clothes- none of which went together, I had asked Issy to find me a bra and he turned up with a lacy strapless one and a pair of Christmas pyjamas!

The Specialist nurse who we now know as Jagoda came in to see us. She gave us a book called 'Joe has Leukaemia' and gave Niamh a toy 'chemo duck' a soft duck which has a portacath in. Both of which Niamh pushed away! Numerous doctors came in and out, we were consented again for LP and chemo and another form for portacath or 'button' as we now refer to it.

At 1400hrs Niamh went to theatre again. She blew me away with how brave she was. It seemed ages to Kev and I how long we were waiting for her to return, as it was a much longer procedure. We saw Geoff in the corridor, and he gave us our first snippet of positive information – there were no leukaemia cells found in her spinal fluid.

I got a phone call from our GP at this time. Geoff had spoken with the surgery that Niamh would *only* be seen at the RVI for the next 2 years. The GP wanted me to know he would do anything he could to help us as a family, and that he remembered seeing Niamh those weeks ago when he had initially requested bloods. It was a heartfelt call that made me emotional again, it didn't take much these days! Eventually after about an hour and a half we were called to theatre. Just as we got there the surgeon that had performed Niamh's surgery was coming out. She stopped to tell us everything was fine however, she had struggled with Niamh's portacath, as she was unable to fit it in the usual place just under the collar bone, because Niamh did not have enough skin to cover there. Hers was therefore placed under her right nipple. Niamh had requested a sausage roll for tea that night but was quite groggy and tired after two days of procedures and didn't eat much.

It was at this time I spoke to a few other parents on the ward. Some were happy to say 'Hello' others did not make eye contact. One lady helped me more than she will ever know. Her son was a teenager and had been admitted at a similar time to Niamh. Coincidentally, she had a daughter also called Niamh! As I mentioned this measuring excrement, I had now found out that when I went to the sluice to put the bowl in there was a marker pen on the side, I had to write Niamh's name on the papier-mâché bowl so that the nurses knew who's it was. As you can imagine this was not the nicest of tasks and I concealed this job from Kev as I didn't think he would ever get over it! This lady said she liked to put her sons bowl next to Niamh's to see their names together.

5/2/2020 DAY 3

Niamh woke and was excited for breakfast after not being allowed any for the past 2 days. She was extremely sore with her new portacath 'button' in and attached intravenous line or 'wiggly' as we now affectionately called it! We had another unsettled night with a couple of hours sleep here and there but that's what I was now used to. It was 'World Book Day' and teachers in the hospital came into rooms offering for children to choose a book. Jagoda came to see Niamh again and brought soft, squishy blood pieces which explained to Niamh about platelets, white blood cells, red blood cells and the naughty leukaemia cell. Niamh listened and tolerated Jagoda discussing these however, when asked if she had read 'Joe has Leukaemia' Niamh refused to talk about it or read it!

Niamh was given a second different type of chemotherapy Vincristine or 'Vinc' as we now know it! It seemed barbaric that the nurse wore goggles and an eye shield to administer it and then pushed it into our little girl's vein. My mum and stepdad brought Issy after school. Issy arrived with Niamh's enormous toy unicorn which she kept on her bed at home – not something I would have thought of bringing but Niamh was over the moon! It was probably the longest the girls had been apart, and they were both missing each other. Niamh was delighted to see Issy, and they snuggled up on the bed together where Issy showed her all her snapchat well wishes from friends. It all got a bit much for Niamh, in the room, she asked everyone to go out whilst she used the toilet, then when they were allowed back in, she said she wanted quiet. My mum was obviously keen to speak to me and find out what had been happening she mouthed 'what happened today?' Niamh said, 'STOP!! Grandma I can hear your lips moving'! Kev took my mum and stepdad into a little room off the ward and recited what had been going on. I got about 5 minutes with them before Niamh demanded me back. They stayed in that room about 10 more minutes then went home. Kev took Issy home that night for a bit of normality for her, so she could sleep in her own bed. I felt so guilty that night, my mum and stepdad had drove all that way and Niamh wouldn't let them near her. Niamh went to sleep, and I rung my mum apologising she said, 'We would drive to the end of the earth for her'. My stepdad said if that was her only form of control, he was happy for her to control them.

6/3/2020 – 8/3/2020 DAYS 4,5,6

Niamh was very poorly over the Friday, Saturday, Sunday, vomiting all the time not really getting out of bed, only for the toilet, and not eating anything. We had been given a special wash we had to use daily, and this became a real struggle. She was sleepy and lethargic, not interested in anything. She would only drink water. Outside of our room was a stand with all the feeds on that go through a feeding tube. Niamh constantly baulked over these, if the door was left open, and therefore it had to be shut most of the time, she was obsessed that she would never have a tube up her nose.

The specialist nurse and consultant were both off for a long weekend. We were so concerned, 'Is this normal?' We had seen other consultants on the ward. One of whom was very loud and jolly and came in one morning shouting, 'Niamh how are you today?'

She looked at him, put her hand up and said, 'Just please go away!!' I was so embarrassed, but she just couldn't be bothered with anyone. He kindly changed her anti-sickness medication and that seemed to improve her greatly. Niamh also asked if she could try tablets rather than medicine suspension, they were surprised with her age but said we could try. Since having her button and wiggly in she had been attached to fluid and a machine that beeped regularly, especially during the night. She hated this so we called it her 'doggy' and would refer to it as such when she was going to the toilet etc. At this time, we were not allowed to mention food at all to Niamh as she would get upset. Niamh decided she would refer to it as 'nothing'! Not the easiest word to pick, but we made it work and occasionally had a giggle over it.

It was during one of these long nights I asked a nurse when Niamh would be able to do normal things again, like go back to school. She said, 'Oh it will be after six months for that'. SIX MONTHS!!! These seemed unimaginable to me - how could we manage? Would I not be able to go back to work? However, little did we know what was around the corner in the form of a worldwide pandemic!

Also, on Saturday 7th Niamh had another chemotherapy added in Pegaspargase (peg) this was given as an injection into the top of her leg. It seemed barbaric all she was going through, then a chemo needed to be given as an injection. I asked why? She had a port in couldn't it be given through this? However, it was explained that research shows this is the best way to give it, as an intramuscular injection, as they can have lower dosage that way and not as often.

Night times were a lonely time! When texting Jo, one of my good friends, she decided we needed a focus and created 'Niamh's Team' to fundraise. The first idea was to run the 'Race for Life'. It's a good job some of my friends worked shifts as my mind worked overdrive and it was impossible to sleep. They would text me throughout the night on nightshifts making me smile with funny stories and keeping my spirits up. Kev and Issy spent time between home and hospital, one of our good friends cooked lots of meals and sent them round – the most thoughtful and fantastic idea.

9/3/2020 DAY 7

I have now lived in hospital for a week and not been home once! Sleep deprivation was the worst - a nurse, one night, had said to me, 'Is it like having a newborn again?' - no not for me! Both my girls had been great sleepers and Niamh slept through the night from seven weeks old! Nothing had prepared me for this, nurses coming in every hour often for either a medication or observation check. I often wondered to myself could they not time the medications better. I eventually discussed this after one night Niamh was woken 7 times for meds and they agreed they could change some timings.

On the clothes front, luckily, my friend Mel had been out and bought me some t shirt bras and the girls from work had come to hospital at the weekend armed with new pjs and smellies. However, my roots now needed colouring and my gel nails all needed to come off – hospitals really need hairdressers and nail technicians!

The consultant and Jagoda were back. They came to see Niamh and asked why she hadn't been walking to the play area! At this time, I couldn't comprehend this…how could she walk to the play area, she could barely get to the toilet, and she had been vomiting, with no food, for three days. They decided they would stop her intravenous antibiotics and fluids and we could finally get rid of 'doggy'. Another nurse came in and said now that Niamh was no longer on antibiotics, she could go into a bay area with three other patients. This was upsetting and worrying as she had just come off antibiotics for neutropenic sepsis, her neutrophils were still only 0.02 and now we were to be sharing a room with possibly six other people (children & parents). I got very upset - lack of sleep for a week! They explained another child may be septic or need isolation – well, what can you say? My child is the most important to me, however, they have a whole ward of sick children to consider. Luckily there was only one other family in the room with us. As Niamh and I weren't sleeping much we went to bed early however, our neighbours in the bed over the way who introduced themselves as Lexie and her mum Suzie were regular visitors to the ward and had Coronation Street playing. Niamh and I had often admired Lexie's lovely River Island silk pjs she wore, as she had walked past our room. Niamh had commented how beautiful she looked with no hair and was envious of her various pjs and we talked about how good they were having buttons down the front to easily attach any drips needed. During the night when Lexie's machine began to bleep Niamh said. 'Push that buzzer, tell them I don't like this room!'

10/3/2020 DAY 8

Home day! After our night in the shared bay both Niamh and I were determined to go home. I got up and dressed in joggers and a hoodie, by this point makeup was no longer essential. Jagoda came to see us and said, 'Mum looks tired, like she needs to go home!'. Niamh needed platelets and the closest ones were in hospital three hours away. I encouraged Niamh to walk to the playroom. It was a struggle after so many days in bed. I could tell she didn't want to go. There was a lady doing music – not the quiet room we had expected! One of the play therapists painted Niamh's nails, then she went back to bed. Kev came and the nurse came round to say they were ordering Niamh's discharge medications and said, 'You look tired today' to me. I said to Kev 'I must look really bad today – she is the second person who has said that!' Kev said, 'You always look beautiful to me.' Something I will never forget!

I was worried about going home – eight days ago I hated it here, now I felt safe. Would I be able to look after Niamh at home? There would be no buzzer for either of us to push! We were taught how to give all Niamh's medications (2 big bags full) and what time to give them. We had to watch a video on how to take care of Niamh at home and how we would need to take her temperature twice a day and the signs for us to become concerned. Jagoda came and said she wanted to show us where we would have regular visits to the day unit. This would begin with twice a week, hopefully soon going to once a week. Niamh was pushed by Jagoda in a wheelchair round to the day unit as she was too frail to walk. Niamh didn't think much of the day unit either and told me, 'I won't be coming back there' – I didn't burst her balloon just yet!

11/3/2020 DAY 9

Our first day home. I felt so much better, a night in my own bed, back with Kev and Issy. Although things were different, Kev was sleeping on the floor in Niamh's room. We could not leave her as she was still unsettled during the night and up and down to the toilet. She was extremely weak and that became more obvious when we got home, we had to carry her up and down the stairs. She just laid on the sofa all day, not wanting to do anything. She watched 'Horrid Henry' all the time. Niamh was still nauseous a lot of the time, although, they had told us her appetite would increase massively with the steroids. However, that didn't happen to Niamh until a good week after starting them. Kev and I were obviously off work 'sick'. We had lots of friends and relatives texting and ringing, wanting to come over. Issy was still going to school as normal. When she got home the girls would cuddle up together and sometimes look at Niamh's messages on snapchat from all her friends, sometimes play a game if she felt up to it or Issy would just sit with her watching 'Horrid Henry'.

At this time the country was just beginning to be warned about COVID-19 we needed to be even more careful. We knew Niamh had no resistance at this time, Kev spent his first few days sourcing any antibacterial products he could, along with toilet rolls and pasta that seemed to be going out of stock quickly. In true Kev style, he came back home armed with quite a collection of goods that lasted us for some time! Niamh's wiggly was still in as we were back at hospital the next day, so they had decided to leave it in. This caused problems as I wanted to give her a lovely bath after getting out of hospital, but we were unable to get it wet, so I was only able to put a small amount of water in the bath. Niamh was able to sit tonight and let Issy do her hair in lovely plaits, after it had been tied in a messy bun, out of her way, all the time we were in hospital.

I carried out a very important task packing a hospital bag. This was to be left in the boot of the car, for any unplanned emergency admissions' I had learnt how necessary this was due to the previous "bra situation".

Niamh's Team had escalated with family, friends, classmates signing up to run 10k the following September. It was astonishing to see the amount raised was already over £6000.

12/3/2020 DAY 10

Back at hospital. First time on the day unit. First impressions it was sooo busy! The teachers were there, they had a band come in which was very noisy in the small, enclosed environment and I felt like I wanted to escape, I can't imagine how Niamh felt! She was quiet, snuggled into me and Kev and wouldn't make eye contact with anyone let alone talk to them, she was extremely withdrawn. We were here for theatre again. Another parent came up to her and asked if she was having a magic sleep, Niamh said 'yes' – I think she could tell she had recently been diagnosed – she gave Niamh £2 and told her to get some sweets after she had been so brave in theatre. People were so kind.

Niamh would be having a bone marrow and lumbar puncture with intrathecal chemotherapy and also Vincristine chemotherapy through her wiggly. She had to have her bloods done first when we got there, and they did this as a finger prick test, another needle into the end of her finger. I couldn't understand this as she had her wiggly still attached surely, they could get blood from there, but apparently it was quicker this way. Niamh was starved again from 7am, and not happy as the steroids had finally kicked in and her appetite was much better, typically she wanted to eat again when she couldn't! We were called in to see Geoff in one of the rooms and he told us that her platelets were low again so she would need a transfusion. This would be her third platelet transfusion in a week. HOW LIFE SAVING IS BLOOD? This got us both thinking how much we would encourage everyone to give blood as it was a major factor in treating Niamh. We both signed up to blood donation. Unfortunately, I was not allowed as I had a transfusion myself when I gave birth to Niamh, however, Kev was and signed up for the next day to give blood.

Niamh was given Vinc again when her wiggly was put in and the platelets arrived prior to going to theatre for the 'magic sleep'. Niamh was tired, hungry and upset. Jagoda came round and encouraged us to put her on a bed in the waiting area. We got her settled and they put the platelets up, quite soon after Niamh complained she was itchy and started to scratch her arms. I asked if they had any Piriton? They rushed in to look and treat it as an anaphylaxis reaction. They gave her antihistamines and steroids through her port and took the rest of the platelets down. It is much more common to have a reaction to platelets than to blood as the testing is not quite as rigorous with platelets. This meant theatre was now cancelled for Niamh! We were concerned that Niamh was missing out on her treatments, but they assured us it would make no difference doing it the week after. The reaction worsened before it got better. Niamh's whole body was red, blotchy, itchy and swollen, but she could now eat so she was happy! There was lots of talk about spending the night in hospital, which I really didn't want to do - luckily the reaction improved quickly and the wiggly finally came out and we were allowed home. The first night I was able to have a proper bath!

13/3/2020 DAY 11

I was actually able to see my mum and aunty! They came over for a coffee. Niamh was settled on the sofa, and we were able to talk in the other room. Also, Mel popped in which was lovely although everyone went through a 'decontamination' procedure when coming in the house as Kev was obsessed with Niamh's immunity being so low.

Kev gave blood and came home with bigger plasters on than Niamh had on for her chest port, which made us all laugh. Issy went to cheer and the cheer girls all videoed a dance for Niamh that she had made up to her favourite song 'Shotgun'. Niamh said it was good, but they didn't do the dance properly, and she would teach them when she was better!

14/3/20 - 15/3/20 DAYS 12,13

Passed without incidents, just lots of Horrid Henry! Issy was at cheer, and I took her and picked her up. I managed to go for a quick coffee with the girls from work on the Saturday and Andrew & Mel came over on Saturday night. I actually had a glass of wine. I was too worried to have more than one as we religiously had to check Niamh's temperature morning and night. We had strict rules if it was more than 37.5, we had to ring the unit or ward. Also, we had now ordered a new bed for Niamh which had a trundle bed below so that we were not sleeping on the floor. She was still very sore and bruised all over her chest. We had promised Issy a bedroom makeover so, as we had emptied her room in preparation for the decorator, she had moved into the playroom.

16.3.2020 DAY 14

Back to Newcastle! They wanted to check Niamh's bloods again. Jagoda just came out and said they were all fine and we could go home. Nice quick visit, we were to learn not many would be like this. Niamh still wasn't walking very well; we were taking her into hospital in an old buggy. She hated it and said she felt people were looking at her, but it was a big hospital and quite a walk from the car to the unit, there is no way she would have managed walking. Also, she was still leaning over to her right side when walking to protect where it was sore over her port. Sleeping was a problem too she could only lay on her left side due to pain all down her right side from her port. Back home to watch more Horrid Henry and a new 'YouTube' favourite 'Dadvgirls!'

17/3/2020 DAY 15

Days spent on the sofa. COVID had hit UK! COVID-19 is a new strain of coronavirus, first identified in Wuhan City, China in December 2019. It was a rapidly evolving situation with a current risk to the UK. We had to make the decision for Issy to stop going to school and cheer as it was too risky that she may contact anything.

It was Mel's 40th birthday. Luckily, I was organised and had got her present. I dropped it on her doorstep. We wouldn't have believed that months later this is the only way of getting things to one another. Niamh was pleased to have Issy home, but also easily got frustrated with her, a side effect of the steroids. Niamh would become moody, angry and teary. We had a visit from Grandma and Grandad. Niamh had got a jigsaw from one of her friends and sat up at the table to do this.

18/3/2020 DAY 16

Issy started her home schooling. Her school were very supportive of our decision to take her out and sent lessons home, sometimes she was able to log into lessons (something that again would become 'normal' when schools later closed due to Covid). Another day on the sofa for Niamh, she also started 'story time' with Papa and Nanny in Spain. They would ring at 4pm and read to her. Sometimes she would fall asleep. Spain was on complete lockdown, at this stage, but not much had changed in the UK, although we had already self-isolated due to Niamh's vulnerability. When Issy was brushing Niamh's hair we noticed lots started to come out. We had been told that Niamh would lose her hair but most likely in a few months I am not sure that any of us were prepared for it come out as quick as it did. I shushed Issy not wanting Niamh to know however, deep down I am sure she did. We had been told it would become itchy and brittle, I definitely wasn't prepared for this to happen yet such a bold sign of chemotherapy treatment.

I had an appointment to get a wisdom tooth removed but had to cancel.

19/3/2020 DAY 17

Another day at the RVI. Niamh starved again from 7am, in preparation for another magic sleep and Vinc. The steroids had properly kicked in now and Niamh and I got up at 6 to have breakfast. She had her cereal but was still hungry, so this was followed by a yoghurt. She then said, 'You know what I really want'? I asked, 'What?', she replied, 'Spaghetti Bolognese'! So, she sat at 6.30am and ate a bowlful of spag bol! When we first went into the unit, we were told only one of us would be allowed to come with Niamh from now on. This was a complete shock! Although we knew about the seriousness of COVID it seemed unimaginable that I would be expected to bring Niamh on my own, to these appointments, having to take her to theatre, watching her go under anaesthetic and Kev not being there. How would I even drive here? I am a competent driver but had let Kev take over on that front from the start of all this. Watching your child being put to sleep was awful and an experience that never got any easier, maybe it would after 2 years of it! Vinc was given again, and her bloods showed she needed a blood transfusion today. The blood transfusion was put up and at about 2.30pm she was taken to theatre. When she came back from theatre, we had to wait quite a while as the blood transfusion had not finished and then after it had, we had to wait an hour longer to ensure no reaction. The bone marrow proved that Niamh's leukaemia had reduced to less than 25% leukaemia cells apparent, exactly the results we were hoping for!

20/3/2020 – 22/3/2020 DAYS 18,19,20

Niamh became stronger as the days went on. She was now able to get up and down stairs. She even managed to do the splits on the sofa. There was a mass at out Parish Church, held for Niamh, but I was unable to attend due to isolating.

On Friday I had booked an appointment with the hairdresser. We had been advised that we should get Niamh's hair cut into a bob as it was much harder if her hair started to fall out whilst it was long. She just didn't feel well enough to have it cut, she didn't want it short either and asked me to cancel. I had already started the process of ordering her a wig as we had been told she would most definitely lose her hair, and the signs were starting to show with even more coming out when we brushed it.

Sunday was Mother's Day; Niamh wrote me a card and made me cry. It was probably one of the hardest days for me to date. I went to see my mum and we had a distanced walk together, but I cried on and off all day. I couldn't really tell you why, I just felt so sad. Sad that our lives had changed so much, sad that Niamh had to go through this. Was it because it was Mother's Day, I'm not sure? Niamh was getting stronger the treatment was working this must be my focus. However, at times it was hard. Also, tonight the news came from the UK Prime Minister, Boris Johnson, that the UK was in lockdown.

Sunday 22ⁿᵈ March 2020

I got diagnosed with leukaemia and then it was coronovirus it was very hard. My Dad got a little too far with hand wash, toilet rolls and pasta, don't ask for anymore stuff! So it began like this......

We went to the hospital and got blood took and we stayed overnight but then the next morning we went to a different hospital and we stayed there for a few nights. then we got to go home for a night, they said it would last for a girl 2 and a half years, but for a boy over 3 years, then we could go home for 4 nights and we went back on Mondays and Thursdays. On Monday I only got a fingerprick, then on Thursday I had to have a magic sleep, it didn't hurt so that was alright but I had to starve. Then we didn't have to go back for another week. So on the next week I only had to have a fingerprick again and just had to have another chemotherapy and this time it was a prick in my butt!

I felt a lot stronger these last few weeks. All my platelets are fine and I'm building up my strength. Tonight I think I am gonna have a nice bath and lay back because my Mum says that if you have a little rest it will help you.

Niamh age 6

23/3/2020 DAY 21

Back to Newcastle, this time just Niamh and I, for her Pegaspargase (peg) injection. I managed to drive on my own and park! Niamh had been up about 6 times for the toilet during the night. Kev and I were concerned that she may have a urine infection. Bloods were done again, and they added on a glucose test when I expressed my concerns. Niamh was asked to do a urine sample too. Her urine showed no infection but lots of glucose and this was confirmed when her blood sugar came back as 30! A normal blood sugar is between 3-7. I was concerned from a nursing point of view. This was scary! They did other blood tests for her pancreas and liver as her stomach was very swollen and she was getting lots of pain. Jagoda reassured us that it was just the steroids (Dex), and it would come down when she finished them. However, for now, we were asked to drastically reduce her sugar intake. My first thought was how will I do this? she was staving all the time and craved jelly sweets and fruit, but it had to be done. I did not want any other interventions if I could help it. I certainly did not want her to start having to inject insulin. After finding out her bloods were fine, they went ahead and gave her peg injection. We had to stay for an hour after that before we were allowed to leave. I explained to Niamh about how she was going to have to omit sugar from her diet. She was upset, but as focused as I was, if it was to help her feel better. We always knew Niamh was strong minded, but her willpower to overcome this, especially during her time of huge steroid input, was immense.

24/3/2020 – 25/3/2020 DAYS 22,23

These days were taken up trying to source 'sugar free' products in the middle of lockdown when we couldn't go out. Lots of friends helped, buying, and sending sugar free varieties of anything they could get. She was starving all the time, due to steroids, and often ate 6 meals a day however, she never once moaned that she couldn't have the things she wanted most. Heart-breaking day! Tuesday, I washed Niamh's hair on Monday night after hospital and on Tuesday morning I couldn't get a brush through it. It looked like it had just tied itself in knots and gone completely brittle. My friend's mum is a hairdresser and armed with gloves and antibacterial sprays galore she kindly came over. It took 5 hours of her cutting and spraying to finally get all the knots out. Niamh sat and let her do it, although the pain must have been intense. At the end she had a very thin bob of hair left with bald patches. Throughout this whole time there are lots of occasions where I was proud of Niamh, but I was extremely proud of her for both of these things. It was a very difficult day it took hours and Niamh was completely worn out! She looked so different already just 20 days after starting treatment the effects of the treatment were making huge physical changes to her appearances.

Tuesday 24th March 2020

The next morning I was up and about, I am getting much stronger so I don't get too worried as it will be fine, but last night I felt quite sick. Then a bit of hair fell out, but it will grow back soon so don't worry. Today I am really excited because I am getting a hair cut. Last night I washed my hair and it is all knotty, but don't worry it will grow back beautiful and you can even get a wig if you like. I am going to get a long bob and when it is all gone we will have a wig for it. When your Mum and Dad is measuring your head you might not like it because I didn't like it, but they need to do it. Once your hair is all gone you can just put a wig on straight away. Just to let you know it would be better if you get your hair done before and don't wash it and be careful with it. We didn't know this and due to it being all knotty it pulled a lot and took a long time to do it.

Niamh age 6

26/3/2020 DAY 24

Another Thursday spent at hospital. The ward was unrecognisable to a week ago. All chairs were spaced out with 2 metres apart, no school or play activities happening now! Vinc again today. I explained to Jagoda about Niamh's hair she said none of the drugs she is on should cause her to lose it. However, since meeting lots of other parents and children on the unit they have said the same thing happened to them in induction.

There were some concerns about one of Niamh's back teeth, so we were referred to a dentist at the RVI, who would be contacting us to make an appointment. The steroids were by now having big effects on Niamh's body, her tummy and face were swollen and bloated and her arms and legs had gone spindly and lost all muscle tone. This upset her daily especially when trying to find clothes to fit and would continue to for some time to come. When I got home today the dentist phoned me to say they would see me the next day at the RVI, another trip!

The clap for 'our NHS' started tonight, we of course joined our neighbours and clapped for my amazing colleagues (who I wished I was beside helping) and the outstanding staff at the RVI treating Niamh.

Thursday 26th March 2020

Today I had to go for an xray on my tooth. It didn't hurt, but not everyone needs an xray but I had to. I need to have a filling. We went to the dentist hospital and I got really bored, tired and very hungry. My Dad bought me 20 chicken nuggets and I ate 10 to myself, my Mum said it's the steroids!

Niamh age 6

27/3/2020 DAY 25

Kev drove us to the dental hospital at RVI. He waited in the car as he wasn't allowed in. Niamh and I were ushered in by receptionists wearing masks. We had to have our temperatures taken before we were allowed in the doors. The dentist was concerned about her tooth at the back, she took an x-ray of it and explained it was an adult back tooth and it was showing slight decay. However, due to Niamh's treatment it was too much of a risk to fill it and she therefore needed to extract it. Not only that one, the one adjacent to it at the top also to level it out. The dentist was going to liaise with the oncology unit and wanted to do it when Niamh was next in theatre, the following Thursday! I was worried about this, another thing for her to go through!

28/3/2020 – 29/3/2020 DAYS 26,27

Another weekend with nothing to do, nowhere to go. As the country was on national lockdown, we had been advised by Niamh's consultant we could not even go out for a walk, we needed to stay isolated in the house. On Sunday there had been a planned mass for Niamh in our church. We are a Catholic family and faith means a lot to us, especially currently. Church services had now ceased due to

Corona and schools were closed. We watched the mass broadcast at home via 'YouTube' with our own candles set out. It was strange with only the priest present.

Little bits of Niamh's personality were reappearing. The day before I had gone to the garage to do a gym workout, I had given her my phone and she was texting my dad in Spain 'Hi are you ok? I'm ok if you want to know' Dad thought it was me sent back 'Hi Tor yes, we are fine thanks.' Niamh replied, 'Its Niamh not your dotter,' which made us giggle!

30/3/2020 – 31/3/2020 DAYS 28,29

Niamh probably had her best day since diagnosis today. She was really good not eating any sugar products although she did love savoury things at this time. One day I made 6 bacon sandwiches!! My friend brought round an enormous cake, left on the doorstep of course, that she had bought for Niamh as it was her birthday on the following Wednesday. Niamh was so excited to have a piece of it as I had said she definitely could have a treat on her birthday. My cousin delivered some sugar free cookies, and I took a gorgeous picture of Niamh enjoying them. This was shared with 'Niamh's Team' as it was uplifting to see her smiling!

1/4/2020 DAY 30

Niamh's 7th Birthday! Not how we had hoped to spend it as she couldn't see anyone. However, we received so many deliveries and she was one spoilt little girl! Her cheerleading teacher had also organised all her team and coaches to record a happy birthday message and sent it to her. This was amazing for her to watch, she loved it! A double celebration as Niamh finished her last dose of steroids today! Yippee it had been a long 28 days and the side effects we had seen were huge. Whenever you speak to any parent with a child going through this, they will all say, 'Steroids are the worst!' THEY ABSOLUTELY ARE! But we must look at what they do for our children, these medications that make them feel so awful, sad and angry are all the time boosting their bloods, when the chemo is rapidly depleting them! They stop them needing more and more transfusions of bloods and platelets. Niamh's hair was thinning more every day, we had ordered her a wig from the 'Little Princess Trust' and were all excited for it to come.

Wednesday 1st April

I didn't have to go to hospital on Monday and I was pleased as it was my birthday on Wednesday. There were a lot of birthday's coming up. There was my Uncle Jonathon's and they had just had baby Abi, my Uncle Paul's and my Mum's. So it was hard but after my birthday I could stop taking my steroids. if you don't know what steroids are they make you feel angry and very, very hungry. Probably you will already know what steroids are, I didn't but I got really hungry and tired. I was very tired during the day but I did try not to go to sleep, but sometimes I just have a little close of my eyes. Feeling sad, angry, tired and hungry, sometimes you will get really tired and really bored, if I had a sleep I often felt a bit better.

I often felt very sickly, I took medicine to help with this. I felt much better after taking my anti sickness tablets. I take tablets but you might take medicine, so I wrote medicine.

Niamh age 7 (today)

2/4/2020 DAY 31

Niamh needed to be last on the list for theatre as the dentist also had to come to remove the teeth. This meant that although she had been starved since 7am she didn't go to theatre until 5pm! When she came back it was so late the day unit had closed so she had to be taken back to a bed on the ward, to be observed for an hour. She didn't even whinge about the pain in her teeth and just started to eat her packed lunch like nothing had happened. Her blood sugar was still high although Jagoda reassured me it would improve now the steroids have stopped; I can't say I was totally convinced about this, but I was to be proved wrong. Her bloods themselves were amazing though. Her platelets, haemoglobin, neutrophils, and white cell count all looked about normal; however, this was to be short lived! Niamh was to start a new chemo medication today, soon to become the most dreaded by us all. 6mp or Mercaptopurine had to be given after one hour starving then followed by another hour starving, every day. The advice was to give it on a night as any dairy products should be avoided (i.e. on a morning they may have cereal with milk). However, this did not work for us as, Niamh, like I'm sure many other children, would eat lots of dairy all day long, she loved yoghurts and glasses of milk.

3/4/2020 DAY 32

Niamh was sore after theatre, so a day spent on the sofa. More 'Horrid Henry'!

Niamh had nearly lost all her hair when her wig arrived! We were all so excited but that didn't last long as the wig was nothing like Niamh's hair had been. As we had discussed it all over facetime and messages the lady had got the colour completely wrong. It was so dark in comparison to what her hair had been like. Niamh took it very well and we had a laugh that she looked like her friend, Lucia, with it on! Niamh put the wig on and her and Issy recorded some 'TikTok's'. Kev and I even joined in, isolation was definitely getting to us!

Always having to be prepared and remembering, on a night, to give 6mp after an hour starving.

4/4/20- 5/4/20 DAYS 33,34

My birthday was on the Saturday. A very different birthday like everybody's was at this time. But friends and family sent things and I had a lovely day. Lockdown was now all over the country and we had zoom bingo and quizzes with friends and family. As one of my friends commented, 'Only Vicky could stop the whole world going on holiday as she wasn't able to!' Niamh kept trying to put her wig on, but it never lasted long she just needed to turn her head and it would fall off. The wig upset me as it didn't look like Niamh.

The 6mp was making Niamh nauseous, she was waking about 5am every morning and being quite sick.

6/4/2020 DAY 35

Niamh was poorly today. She laid on the sofa all day. I kept taking her temperature as I just felt 'she wasn't right' but it didn't go up. She slept a lot during the day. I took a picture of her today and I probably felt it was the picture where she looked the most poorly. She wanted to go to bed early we were having an online quiz with Kev's family on the night. Issy went up to see Niamh just before we the quiz finished. Issy said she thought Niamh looked flushed and was concerned so she did her temperature. It was 38.1, anything over 37.5 I had to ring the hospital. The nurse said because it was over 38, I had to attend straight away. As covid was prevalent, we had to go to A&E at the RVI to be assessed first as it could be covid related. I wasn't happy about this! But what could I do? I had to go on my own with Niamh. We got there and had to queue to book in then they took us through to the children's area and we were told to sit in the waiting area. I told the nurse that Niamh was an oncology patient and felt she needed to be in isolation. They agreed with this and put us straight into a room. A nurse did her observations and thankfully her temperature had already dropped. The oncology doctor and nurse then accessed Niamh's port and took bloods, to rule out neutropenic sepsis. We were told we could either go to the ward or wait to see what her neutrophils came back as, because if they were ok, she was not classed as septic neutropenic, and we could go home. We chose to stay there and wait. Everyone was very impressed that Issy had recognised the signs of a raised temperature! We waited for about an hour and a half and eventually her bloods were back, and she wasn't neutropenic! We could go home! The A&E nurse came and removed Niamh's wiggly. Niamh said she wasn't very good at it and she hurt a lot! She said she didn't like the A&E nurses (forgetting I was one)!! We arrived home about 3am.

<pre>
             Thursday 8th April

I got a bit of hayfever. Mummy and I had a
   little sleep, then I had story time with
Nanny and Papa. We are on 'The Faraway Tree'
  I LOVE reading. I got a kindle and an ipad
    for my birthday. We went on facetime for
 story time and my Papa and I read a chapter
  each. Then that night I was sick and very
      tired but then I was a lot better and
   stronger. I had finished my steroids now,
but I was still quite tired. So I would just
         sit on the sofa and watch TV.

                  Niamh age 7
</pre>

7/4/20 - 8/4/20 DAYS 36/37

Niamh was tired and developed a bit of a cough over these days. I rung the ward on the Wednesday to inform them. Also, at the time I had bad hay fever. The nurse on the phone said I might have to take Niamh to A&E again. I couldn't believe it and I felt they were putting Niamh at risk! I got upset on the phone and the nurse said she would get Jagoda to ring me back. Jagoda was as efficient as ever and said we were to go to the ward, but they would put us in a side room. Geoff said he wasn't concerned she had COVID he thought she probably had some hay fever like me and added an antihistamine to our ever-expanding list of medications.

CONSOLIDATION

9/4/2020 DAY 38

We had now officially finished the induction stage and commenced 'consolidation'. Unfortunately, this meant a lumbar puncture for 4 weeks in a row. Niamh had a ptosis (which means droopy) on her left eyelid. Thankfully it didn't last too long and was medication related. We were to find out that if there was a side effect with medication Niamh was likely to get it! She walked from the car to the ward for the first time today. As we approached the ward Niamh said to me, 'This is the place I love to be.' I laughed at her, 'I never thought you would say that!' 'Well,' she replied, 'Rather than A&E after the other night!'

Her bloods were really good today which was a bit of a surprise as 6mp can drop them quite a bit, but Niamh was managing it well apart from the sickness and maintained 100% dose. We also had another bone marrow test which would be sent away to determine the MRD 'minimum residual disease'. This refers to the level of leukaemia in which there are less than one thousand million cancer cells in the body and therefore cannot be detected by a microscope. We were told it would be a few weeks to get this result back.

It was on this occasion we met Billy a little whirlwind toddler running around the ward with his chemo attached. He definitely brought a smile to Niamh's face. He was there with his mum and, seeing as this was the only place us oncology parents were allowed to go, we had a good chat. Billy had ependymoma a type of cancer that develops in the brain or spinal cord. Ependymoma most often occurs in young children, as in Billy's case.

10/4/2020 DAY 39

Niamh was happy to be eating anything she wanted again. Although she didn't really fancy any sweet things still, but it was good to have the choice and she was happy to be able to eat fruit again.

Friday 10th April

I was sitting in the garden, I liked drinking milk and eating cookies. We baked today and made some cheese scones and chocolate cakes. I was able to start going to the toilet myself and I could now walk up and down stairs, I felt like I had a lot of my strength back. We had a little talk about sleeping, I was going to sleep with Issy but instead my Mum slept with me or my Dad.

From my Mum I could get some sickness tablets or medication. Just take it, because if you don't take it you might need to have a tube up your nose. You will start to feel like yourself again and then you wont' be as tired.

Niamh age 7

11/4/2020 DAY 40

Niamh decided that as she was now nearly bald it was only fair that her dad shaved his hair off too. This was a momentous occasion for Kev, he loved his hair and took great pride in styling it every day, so we videoed it whilst Niamh shaved it. After, we all had a good laugh about it and Niamh decided to nominate quite a few of the men in her life to do the same! Issy invented the Shave4Niamh!! In all intents and purposes this was a bit of fun to get us through lockdown and to empower Niamh although it turned into a whole lot more.

12/4/2020 - 15/4/2020 DAYS 41-44

Easter Sunday-my mum had scoured the internet and paid over the odds for what she thought was a sugar free egg for Niamh. She sent it via delivery and was excited on facetime seeing Niamh open it, she was very surprised at Niamh saying it was disgusting. When we looked at the box, she had bought gluten free instead of sugar free!

These days were spent getting videos and pictures of family and friends all supporting Niamh in her 'Shave4Niamh'. Our friend decided to set up a 'GoFundMe' page which became the next fundraiser for 'Niamh's Team' and ask all the men that were shaving their heads to donate their hair cut money for the hospital that was treating Niamh. It had started as some fun but so many people were happy to get involved, we thought we should put it to a good cause.

The 6mp was becoming increasingly problematic as it was later and later that Niamh was going to bed as she was wanting extra food after the second hour of starving – it was a good job she didn't need to be up on a morning!

Thursday 16/4/2020 DAY 45

Back to hospital. We had noticed that Niamh's nose looked like it had a delve in it on the bridge, it looked like a bruise and was quite noticeable. They asked us if she had banged it. She hadn't been anywhere or done anything for her to bang it! They dismissed it saying it should go.

Another day in theatre, as we were waiting, we got talking to a couple of other mums, I explained how much I was struggling with the timing of the 6mp, one of them advised to do it earlier, 2 hours before tea. I decided to see if this worked better for us.

We also met Craig and Reuben at this time. Reuben had ALL the same as Niamh and was on exactly the same treatment, he was diagnosed only two weeks after Niamh. Unfortunately, the harsh induction treatment had caused Reuben to stop using his legs completely and he was needing to use an adapted buggy. Craig joked with Niamh that he had also done the 'Shave4Niamh' as he was bald already!

The journeys home from hospital on my own were probably one of the hardest things about Kev not being able to be there. Especially after theatre Niamh was often quite groggy and sickly. Despite the multiple anti sickness medications, she was taking she would often start vomiting in the back of the car. This meant making sure we were always prepared with lots of sick bowls and tissues, luckily due to COVID the traffic was always minimal but pulling up on the hard shoulder of a motorway was a bit scary!

10/4/20- 15/4/20 DAYS 46-51

More and more people joined in the 'Shave4Niamh' we were stunned to see over £2000 had been raised! Some of our friends from Spain also decided to fundraise and were also raising amazing amounts. Niamh had told her consultant about the fundraising, and we asked where he would suggest the money go to. He suggested the charity 'Children's Cancer North' as that's who supported the oncology wards. Geoff himself got involved too and dyed his hair purple – the colour of leukaemia cells and shaved it off to raise money for the charity.

The 6mp was becoming slightly easier as we all got a bit more used to it and I had moved to the earlier time of before tea, which was working better for us.

16/4/2020 DAY 52

When we went back to the hospital Niamh's nose appeared worse and we mentioned it again. Geoff agreed that the cartilage in her nose was damaged. The ear, nose and throat doctor was called to the unit to see her. He felt the same, the cartilage for some reason was damaged, why? No one knew! It was decided that they had concerns, so they wanted her to have a CT scan and a biopsy in theatre, to rule out there was nothing else underlying or sinister. This was not what I was wanting to hear! Niamh needed to come during the week for the CT, with the biopsy being done the week after, along with her lumbar puncture.

17/4/20-22/4/20 DAYS 53-58

A week of worry followed. The radiologists and radiographers in CT could not believe how brave she was. Niamh got on the machine and just laid still, they said lots of children her age needed to be sedated for a scan. Niamh came off and said it felt like a ride! We wouldn't get any results until we seen the ENT Drs again on the following Thursday. However, Niamh in herself was doing great, her strength was building back up and on the 17th she did her first handstand since she had been diagnosed.

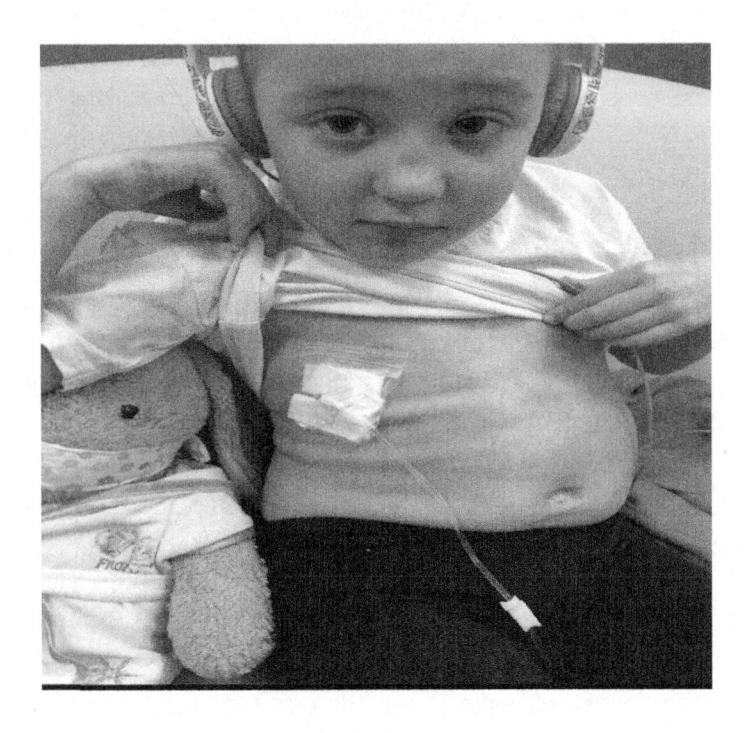

23/4/20 DAY 59

Hospital day! We met many people along our journey. Most of whom made time easier for us on the unit chatting and passing the time. Everyone being so grateful to the doctors and nurses saving our babies lives. A few comments stick in my mind over this time. With Niamh not being long out of induction and quite poorly, a lady with a little boy of about 8 started to talk to me in the waiting room and ask where Niamh was in her treatment cycle. I asked the same about her son, who I commented looked very well in himself. Her reply shocked me she said, 'Yes their hair grows back, and everyone ignores you, it's like he's not even poorly anymore.' I remember thinking to myself - that's the stage I want to get to, where Niamh is no longer distinguished by this illness.

Many others had much harder journeys than ours and Niamh and I often left the unit feeling lucky – what a strange position to be in!

We were seen by both the Oncology and the ENT Consultants today. The first bit of amazing news came from Geoff. Niamh's MRD was back, and it was low risk she had hit remission! We then saw the ENT consultant who explained she had not seen anything of cause for concern on Niamh's CT, however, she still needed to go ahead with an internal examination in theatre. She decided that if there was nothing to see on examination, she would not do a biopsy. She planned to come and see me, either way, after surgery. As before with her dental work she was put last on the list for theatre due to the ENT treatment she needed. Some long, starved hours were ahead for us! Eventually Niamh went to theatre she was there slightly longer than normal but came back and didn't complain about any pain in her nose just started to eat her packed lunch as usual. Quite quickly the ENT Dr came to see me she said on internal examination it was obvious there was some collapsing to the cartilage but no untoward lumps or bumps and nothing that needed further investigation. There was still no explanation for the deformity of the cartilage and the consultant explained she had never encountered it before. She was going to do some research, but the only conclusion was that the high dose steroids had destroyed the cartilage. The ENT Dr offered reconstructive surgery in the future; it was not something we wanted to consider at present. Poor Niamh! Another thing for her to contend with, as usual she did not allow it to bother her. As soon as she got in, she shouted up the stairs to Issy in her bedroom, 'I can have a nose job if I want!!'

24/4/2020 - 29/4/2020 DAYS 60-65

Obviously, we shared our amazing news that Niamh had a low risk MRD therefore meaning that the first stage of her treatment reduced the burden of leukaemia cells to a level which allowed production of normal blood cells to resume. This point is defined as remission. Remission meant to a lot of people Niamh was cured. Unfortunately, in leukaemia this is not the case and there could still be up to as many as one thousand million leukaemia cells in her body and another 2 years of further treatment was needed to completely eradicate the disease from her body. If Niamh was a boy, it would be 3 years of further treatment!

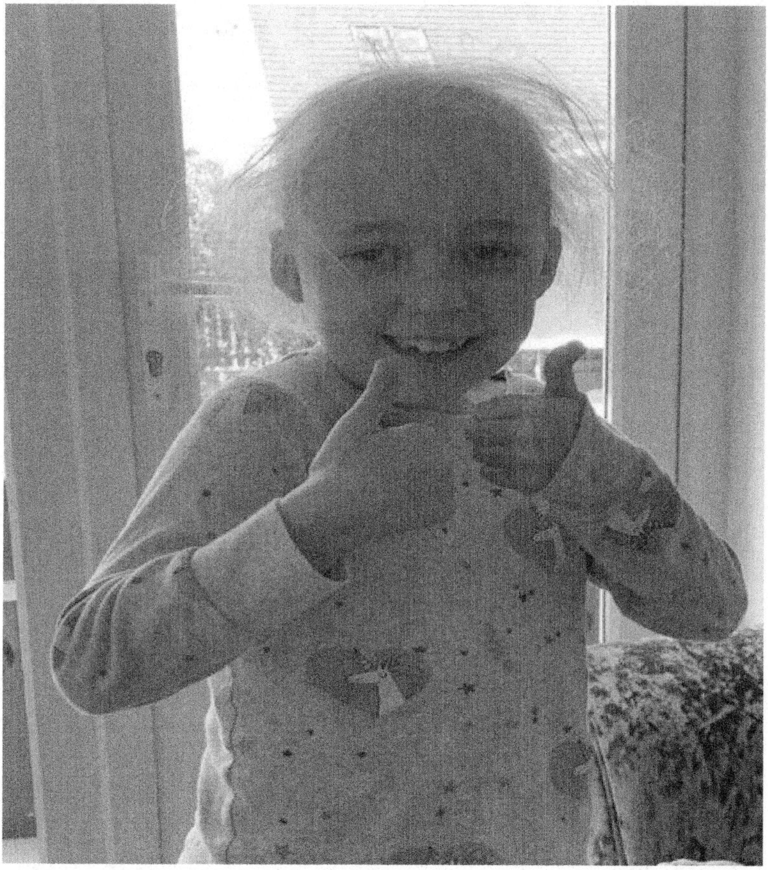

INTERIM MAINTENANCE

30/4/20 DAY 66

We received Niamh's end treatment date today 30/4/2022!! Even though this felt so far away it was a relief to have a date we could concentrate and focus on. A big party date! Niamh was to start 'interim maintenance' today, thank goodness a few weeks break of theatre visits. However, steroids and Vincristine were again starting today along with another oral chemo 'Methotrextate'. The latter would usually be given intratheacally with her lumbar puncture in theatre, in the weeks she did not have LPs she would be given this orally. With all of the worry of Niamh's nose I discussed with Geoff about having steroid treatment again although this time it was only a 5 day course. Geoff felt continuing with the treatment was the most important thing to do.

A surprisingly quick visit after all those weeks of long theatre days! Niamh found her own way of communicating how she felt on steroids around this time, 'I feel like my teeth are angry,' she would say. I think verbalising this made her feel marginally better.

1/5/2020 DAY 67

Today my baby nephew was born in Thailand. This was to be my mum's 3rd grandchild all born on the 1st of the month! A traumatic day as David my brother was in the Ukraine, and it was a difficult birth with Mum and baby being quite poorly. Baby Arthur was sent to intensive care, and it was hard for David to find out much with the language barrier over the phone. Later, we heard that Mum and baby were back together and doing fine.

2/5/2020 – 3/5/2020 DAYS 68-69

Niamh was getting stronger by the day, we went out on a bike ride today, but she wasn't strong enough to ride her bike. Luckily, we still had a baby seat on the back of Kev's bike which she was small enough to fit in. Just getting some fresh air and a change of scenery made her (and us) feel so much better. It had been so hard for Issy not able to go anywhere, see anyone, she had been couped up in her bedroom for 12 weeks! Thank goodness for facetime and mobile phones!

4/5/2020 - 6/5/2020 DAYS 70-72

The weather was lovely, and we started spending a lot of time outdoors as Niamh was now stronger and feeling better. It was our wedding anniversary on 5/5 the girls set the table as if we were in a restaurant, to make tea a little bit special. We were also front page of our local paper, as someone had shared our story about 'Shave4Niamh'. We received more photos everyday of people taking part, it was amazing!

Niamh's grandad, Terry, also decided to give himself a challenge of riding 4000 miles on his bike before his 78th birthday in September.

7/5/2020 DAY 73

This felt like a momentous day. It was a Thursday and no hospital! Through this interim maintenance period we would only need to go to hospital every 2 weeks. Niamh and I enjoyed having a week off.

8/5/2020 DAY 74

VE Day! It had been decided on a message chat from our neighbours that we would do a socially distanced street party. We spent the morning baking scones and cakes then had a lovely couple of hours outside chatting to our neighbours from afar. Kev got the karaoke machine out and Niamh also did a few little songs for everyone. Although she tired quickly.

9/5/2020 - 10/5/2020 DAYS 75-76

We got a couple of little surprises my stepdad had made Kev and I a pallet gin bar for the garden for our anniversary. He put it up in the garden as a surprise this weekend. Also, Issy had contacted Niamh's favourite youtubers without us knowing and they had sent her a personalised video. I don't think I have ever seen Niamh so overwhelmed about anything; she was absolutely over the moon.

11/5/2020 – 13/5/2020 DAYS 77-78

The Zoom quizzes continued! I was still trying to continue with my uni work for my MSc throughout this and finally completed one of this year's assignments and handed it in. Although Niamh was brighter in herself, she wasn't eating very well, unless on her week of steroids. She had started to become quite sickly again, especially on a morning. I felt it was the 6mp! Again, we were back to the starving routine and taking it before going to bed. She began waking most mornings at about 5am, again feeling nauseous, and often vomiting.

14/5/2020 DAYS 79

Back to RVI and another magic sleep! Another long day for us! I mentioned to Jagoda about Niamh being sick early on a morning and she said maybe to try and give her something to eat after the hour she starves after taking 6mp. This was to be easier said than done! Niamh was still maintaining 100% doses which they were really happy about.

Reuben had also joined us on interim maintenance and was on the same two-week cycle as us. He always came to hospital with his dad Craig. Craig was like a walking encyclopaedia on leukaemia I think he might have even been able to give Jagoda a run for her money, all that he had read up on. Rueben was still really struggling to walk due to all the medications. Although Rueben was only diagnosed 2 weeks after Niamh, as a boy, he wouldn't finish his treatment until a full year after Niamh.

15/5/2020 - 17/5/2020 DAYS 80-82

'Shave4Niamh' was still going strong, and we had nearly reached £7000 in this short space of time. Niamh went on the trampoline today and managed to do some 'flicks' and a little show with Issy. She was growing stronger by the day! She was still very sickly on a morning, and it was difficult trying to feed her again after having the 6mp as it was getting so late. She was going to sleep on a night after starving then wanting food. It just wasn't working for us.! I was grateful that she didn't have school as it was becoming 10pm when we would eventually get her to bed.

18/5/2020 - 24/5/2020 DAYS 83-89

An uneventful week. Another week off from the RVI on Thursday. McDonalds opened back up on Wednesday after months of lockdown. Niamh was extremely excited to get one to eat and we queued at the weekend! As you can imagine the whole world had missed McDonalds and the queues to get in the drive through, as the restaurants were still not open, were enormous. Niamh needed a wee whilst we were in the car. Luckily, I had a spare vomit bowl and she had to do a wee in that like a potty! Niamh only managed eating about half after all that trouble!

25/5/2020 - 31/5/2020 DAYS 89-95

Another week of lovely weather. Back at hospital on Thursday for dreaded steroids again and Vincristine. Niamh was still really off her food, and I had started to give her 6mp even earlier starving her for an hour late afternoon, then having 6mp then starving again for an hour, then having tea. This appeared to be working better. Niamh was no longer vomiting but still very nauseous and just not really interested in food. I asked the specialist nurse about giving it even earlier in the day, I was told we could, but milk products must be eliminated for the two hours between having it, which is why they say avoid breakfast as its thought she would have cereal and milk. Niamh loves all things with milk and would often just have a cup of milk to drink, has yoghurts all through the day so I didn't feel a morning would be much different to later on for us! We tried this and got into a much better routine of having it first thing on a morning before eating, then waiting an hour before any food.

1/6/2020 - 3/6/2020 DAYS 96-98

We played lots of games now Niamh was getting stronger and feeling better. These consisted of 'Stop the Bus' and 'Howa Neighbour.' The latter was Niamh's made-up game where one person was on and had to hide 3 items throughout the house the other two had to find them whilst not being caught. Niamh, Issy and I had a lot of laughs playing. Niamh had started to do some home school by now and Issy of course had home school every day too, but both usually finished by lunchtime.

4/6/2020 DAY 99

Back to hospital, back to theatre and magic sleep. Another little girl was in today who was a bit in front of Niamh with her treatment. Niamh and her were able to have a little distanced chat in the waiting room and after theatre, when they were both eating their packed lunches. After starving all day, the kids were always ready for their packed lunches when they got back from theatre. Rueben was also there he had his dummy in and Jagoda came up and said, 'I think he's a bit old for that.' He was only 3 and had just been through a trauma of theatre and starving all day! Niamh and I thought he deserved his dummy, maybe the only thing Niamh disagreed with Jagoda about!

5/6/2020 DAY 100

Niamh was sore today after theatre. Quiet day on the sofa was called for. However, she still managed to do some schoolwork online.

Day 100 today, 100 days of this awful terrifying journey. I don't really think I ever thought why us? Why not? I'm not sure why but I think it's just not worth thinking that. Why anyone! All I focused on is that leukaemia is treatable with amazing outcomes. No child should ever have to go through it, but they do, and they are amazing, so much more resilient than us adults.

Terry had passed the halfway mark on his bike ride of 4000 miles. A great achievement and he was certainly set to hit his target, although he said it was getting harder especially with the hot days we were having.

6/6/2020 -7/6/2020 DAYS 101-102

Another achievement today Niamh ate a full chicken dinner after two weeks of being unable to eat. We also had a few hours outside socially distanced with our neighbours again, after the success of VE Day which we had all enjoyed.

8/6/2020-14/6/2020 DAYS 103-109

A break from hospital this Thursday. We were getting used to this but dreading going into delayed intensification and concerned that she would be very unwell again. Niamh decided she wanted to help others getting diagnosed with leukaemia and set up her own 'YouTube channel' called 'Niamh's Journey'. She recorded it all herself explaining what had happened to her. This was completely her words without any input if you ever watch it, you will see its definitely uncensored!

We would have loved to do something nice at this time as Niamh was so well but unfortunately still being in lockdown nothing was open! The girls had a little belated party at home this weekend as a local party planner delivered a sleepover kit for the girls to enjoy a nice night together. We got some ice creams delivered and all watched a movie. The girls enjoyed a night sleeping in tepees in the lounge, something a bit different.

15/6/2020-17/6/2020 DAYS 110-112

Home schooling continues and on Wednesday the CCLG announced that shielding has now officially stopped! Amazing news for us. It means at last, we could go outside for a walk and even go and sit in my mum's garden and enjoy a catch up. After a long few months this was the best news ever, although all I really wanted was a hug and a kiss from my mum, but this still wasn't allowed! My stepdad had been busy in lockdown having made Niamh an amazing treehouse in their garden. She was so excited to go and play on it.

18/6/2020 DAY 113

Today Niamh had to have an ECHO scan (a scan of her heart) a particular type of chemotherapy that she would start in delayed intensification 'Doxorubicin' can affect the heart, so it is important to get a baseline, prior to starting the medication.

Whilst in the waiting room, I personally felt they had gone a step too far with COVID regulations as they were no two chairs next to each other and Niamh had to sit on my knee! It felt they hadn't considered you could be there together from the same household. The ECHO itself was fine just like an ultrasound scan when you are pregnant.

We spied a little girl in the waiting room today who had gorgeous long hair. Niamh said it brought back memories of when she got diagnosed and she felt sorry for her because she had a needle in her arm! She said, 'I hope she doesn't have leukaemia and lose all that lovely hair'. Little did we know this was Evie and her and Niamh were going to become the best of friends.

19/6/2020 – 21/6/2020 DAYS 114-116

My research assignment, that I had worked hard on, was due in today for my MSc. Uni kept telling me to put a hold on my studies, but I was determined just to get on and do it if possible.

Niamh's friend, Lucia, came round and sat for a little distanced visit outside, as did her friend Erin. She loved seeing them both although, was very quiet. Things were still very worrying with covid and although we were told we didn't have to shield anymore we were still very careful and only seen anyone at a distance and outdoors. That being said, we knew we had a week with Niamh being well prior to starting Delayed Intensification and we didn't want to waste it!

22/6/2020 – 23/6/2020 DAYS 117-119

Every Monday and Tuesday Niamh had to have a special antibiotic twice a day Co-trimoxazole or Septrin as we called it. She had to have it morning and night on these two days every week. It helped to protect her immunity from any bugs going round, as often she had low resistance. Needless to say, since the start of all this my house looked like a pharmacy and I had to remind myself frequently of all the times and days these different medications were needed. Some other parents told me they would set alarms to alert them and later on especially with 6mp Niamh would often ask 'Alexa' to inform her when her hours starving was finished.

On Tuesday we went strawberry picking it was a lovely day and Niamh looked so well. In fact, as one of my friends commented you wouldn't know anything was wrong you would just think she had 'shit hair'!

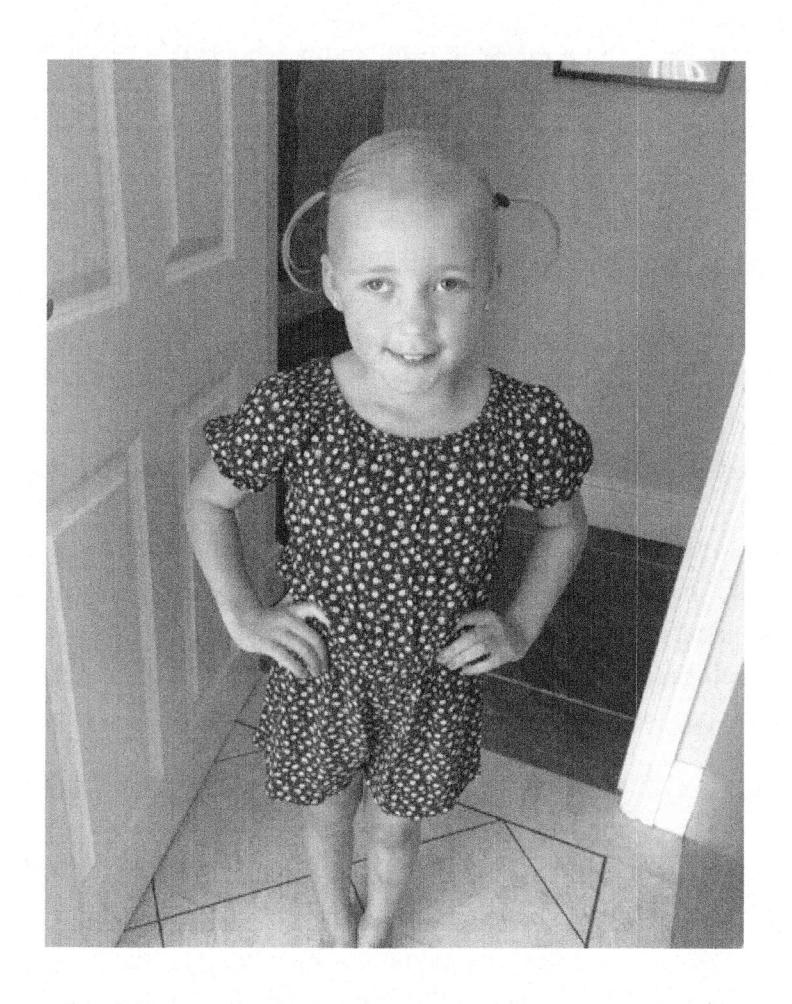

24/6/2020 – 25/6/2020 DAYS 120-121

We had some little walks and nice days in the garden as the weather was still good. Niamh and Issy were doing home schooling daily. Kev's sister, who has a guest house in Fort William, was desperate to see us. She had been closed during the covid pandemic but was hoping to open up the following week. She asked us to go there prior to Niamh starting her next round of treatment. It was a big decision for us as we would be so far from Newcastle Hospital but on the other hand Niamh was so well, we decided to go for it! A change of scenery would do us all good.

On Thursday I got a message from a lady who said her little girl was a similar age to Niamh and they had seen us on ward 14 (the day unit). Her daughter Evie was 8 and had aplastic anaemia – her bone marrow had completely stopped working and they were looking for a stem cell donor. I said that Niamh had commented on Evie's gorgeous hair the other day and that we could hopefully see each other again at the hospital and the girls could meet properly. Masks were now obligatory when visiting the hospital and with a socially distanced waiting room this wouldn't be as easy as expected.

We started allowing Issy to go on some walks with one of her friends. She had been cooped up for so long. It was a worry as the news was all about how the teenage age group were spreading COVID more and deaths were again rising. However, Issy was sensible and missed her best friend Caolan so much. Issy had spent so much time with Niamh and had been like a little saviour to me, but she needed time for herself too, although she never complained!

26/6/2020 – 28/6/2020 DAYS 122-123

We went for it and travelled to Fort William. We had a lovely few days and it made me realise how much Issy had missed out on, these last few months. She loved spending time with her cousins and even jumped in a 6ft waterfall! We had some nice walks, and it was lovely to see Jan and Jamie. Niamh luckily, was extremely well and enjoyed every minute especially taking their dog, Duggie, for walks as she was desperate for a puppy. She had been for a while, but we were told at the beginning of treatment no new pets.

29/6/2020 DAY 124

Niamh's first covid swab (the first of many)! The new rules now were prior to any theatre visits (magic sleeps) a covid swab was necessary. In order for us not to have another visit to the RVI we were able to have it done locally. My boss at work said we could have a drive through test, carried out at our nearest hospital. It wasn't nice and made Niamh's nose bleed. She wasn't happy!

30/6/2020 – 1/7/2020 DAY 125-126

Finally, the hairdressers opened, and I could get a hair appointment! They wouldn't recognise me at the RVI on Thursday without my greys!

Wednesday, a day enjoying Niamh being well and schoolwork completed. We were all quite apprehensive about the upcoming visit on Thursday at the hospital and starting delayed intensification (DI). We had been prepared that this could be the worst stage treatment.

DELAYED INTENSIFICATION

2/7/2020 DAY 127

Started delayed Intensification. I was very worried about this stage, some people said this was the worst of all the treatment. Others said induction prepares their bodies for this and therefore it is not so bad. However, they prepare you for the worst. What a day, Vincristine, steroids, magic sleep and a new medication Doxyrubicin or the 'red devil' as people name it! This new chemotherapy is bright red and will turn their wee and tears red. This is the chemo that will turn them shiny bald, and Niamh would lose those little tufts of hair she still liked to put in bunches. Her hair had just started to grow back, and she had a small covering over her head from interim maintenance, but this was all to go again. Starved again with lots of anti-sickness and pain medication on board, as the nurses had advised it would be a long wait for her magic sleep. She was in good spirits though. As for the mask wearing it was AWFUL! They had become more lenient with the kids and said anyone under 12 didn't have to wear one. All I wanted to do was comfort her and give her a kiss, when she was crying in the ward getting yet another needle into her chest and more chemotherapy, and I'm unable to as I'm wearing a mask! As parents we must wear them and wait for often over 8 hours waiting for different types of treatment. It made me angry and upset when I heard people complaining about putting them on in a shop!

Craig and I complained all day about the masks, it was hard when you wanted to gesture or mouth something you didn't want the kids to hear – this was no longer possible.

3/7/2020 DAY 128

Niamh amazed me today she was on great form even after all that medication yesterday, I couldn't believe it. She really is a true warrior and her resistance amazed me.

4/7/2020 – 5/7/2020 DAYS 129-130

The delayed effect started today! Niamh was wiped out all weekend. She kept falling asleep and the steroid effect where she always needed me close, and feelings of sadness loomed over her. In this round she had to have 7 days of an even higher dosage of steroids then 7 days break then another 7 days steroids again. It was going to be a tough few weeks for us all. On the 4th July, national lockdown lifts and things reopened. We weren't in a rush to go anywhere but I was pleased things were getting back to normality, a very new normal!

6/7/2020 DAY 131

Another day at the RVI but also a day to celebrate Niamh's last Peg injection! Niamh was so brave she didn't even have cold spray on, despite feeling a bit grotty still. However, it made Niamh feel a lot better that Evie was there again. They started to chat, this was nice and passed the time a bit quicker. When we got home Erin (Niamh's best friend) rung Niamh on facetime to give her some news that she was going to get her very long hair cut off and donate it to the 'Little Princess Trust' who had donated Niamh's wig.

We also decided we wanted something to look forward to today, so we booked a Christmas weekend at Center Parcs.

7/7/2020 – 8/7/2020 DAYS 132

We had some lovely weather and the girls had ordered a new enormous trampoline. Kev and I put it up and the girls loved playing on it. Niamh's strength had built up massively in interim maintenance however, it was now starting to deplete again. At this time, some of our friends had been selling bands with 'Niamh's Team' on (not the easiest thing to do in lockdown). They had made an astounding amount and donated it to 'Niamh's Team'! Also, a local lady made little craft teddy bears and put a donation pot outside her house. She came round and gave Niamh a cheque for the money she had raised. People were so kind and generous!

9/7/2020 DAYS 133

Back again to the RVI for the second dose of Doxyrubicin and another dose of Vincristine. One week off steroids, hurray! We were ready for that! Evie was there again, and the girls were becoming firm friends as they had lots of similar interests.

10/7/2020 – 12/7/2020 DAYS 134-136

Niamh was on great form this weekend even after all the chemo she had been given in the past 10 days! She perfected her first roundoff back handspring again on the trampoline. We also had a little, socially distanced outside, street party with the neighbours. The kids took part in a little sports day and Niamh won a few prizes. She continued to surprise us all.

13/7/2020 DAY 137

There was a transition day at school today just for two hours. Niamh was apprehensive but had wanted to go if she was well enough. We had asked Geoff, on Thursday, if it was possible as she was neutropenic at the moment. He said if she felt well enough, to let her attend. As she had been on such good form the past few days she was wanting to go. As we pulled up in the car park she became quite upset and told me she was worried about how she looked. I told her she looked beautiful as always and off she went. I was very proud of her for going in and being really brave. Another tear sprung to my eyes. What a milestone for her to achieve, I think around this time all children and parents were a little apprehensive about them mixing again back at school, however, for Niamh this was enormous. She came back happy and exhausted and needed a lay down after only 2 hours at school but was so pleased to have seen all her school friends and teacher.

14/7/2020 - 15/7/2020 DAYS 138-139

We went for little walks as Niamh was so well. We tried to get out as much as possible after all those months of not being allowed out of the house! Niamh's hair had started to grow again which was a great sign it would come back in long-term maintenance (LTM).

16/7/2020 DAY 140

RVI day. Another Vincristine, Doxyrubicin and the dreaded Dexamethasone steroids for another 7 days.

For my MSc I had an online seminar after getting back from the hospital, so a very long day!

17/7/2020 DAY 141

This is the day schools should have broken up for the summer holidays. It seems a lifetime ago they were there, and things were normal.

Niamh was back to 'steroid Niamh' today very sad and upset, not herself at all. It was incredible how she could go from my bubbly little girl to a sad and needy child in just a few hours.

18/7/2020 DAY 142

Cheerleading started back today, Niamh had been so excited but had been unwell the night before and ended up sleeping with me. After a very unsettled night she was still fast asleep when I took Issy to cheer this morning! Niamh was so disappointed as well as feeling low from the steroids- not a good combination! This wore her out and she slept on and off on the sofa all day. Days like this were just the saddest, she felt so low and there was little I could do to help her.

19/7/2020 DAY 143

Niamh felt much better this morning, so we went for a walk at the Barrage, it was a lovely day. However, she felt people were looking at her, got upset and wanted to go home. When we got home, she slept on the sofa for hours. I was told the steroids make them quite awake and hyper however, they just wiped Niamh out!

20/7/2020 DAY 144

Erin had her big hair cut today! Niamh was meant to go and watch but she wasn't well enough. Erin recorded it for her and was really pleased she donated it to the 'Little Princess Trust' and raised over £1000! She also loved her new hair in a bob. What a generous, selfless thing to do! The girls were the best of friends and couldn't wait to be able to see more of each other again, they both missed each other terribly. When Niamh felt up to it, they would have facetime calls and often do 'spa' evenings where they would both put a facemask on and chat online.

21/7/2020 DAY 145

We started to see a few friends in the coming days of nice weather. This seemed to take Niamh's mind off feeling so bad but also wore her out and daily she would have a sleep through the day. Kev and I went out for our first meal together and a couple of hours to ourselves, it was lovely and just what we needed after all this time.

22/7/2020 DAY 146

Kev was allowed to come to the hospital today. Jagoda had asked us to come on the Wednesday rather than the Thursday as Niamh didn't need any treatment this week. We were to have a teaching session on Cytarabine, the next chemo that Niamh would need next week. However, it had to be administered through her wiggly 4 days in a row which meant, if parents agreed, they would leave her wiggly in and the parents would give the medicine at home. If we couldn't do it, we would have to attend the hospital every day.

I wasn't too worried about learning to do the intraport medication, with being a nurse, it was very in depth, and I felt like I was back at nursing school again. Jagoda was pleased with me though, which was high praise indeed! Kev thought he didn't have a part in it however, Jagoda assured us it was a double act, and he must take part which Niamh found really amusing……it was nice to see her cheeky smile again after the week of steroids.

Today was also the day we had our holiday booked and should have all been travelling to Newcastle Airport, instead of hospital, to go to Spain! It felt like it would be a long time until we would be able to go abroad again.

23/7/2020 – 26/7/2020 DAYS 147-150

Steroids finished now until we hit maintenance…woohoo!!

My friend had a little afternoon tea for a few of the work girls. Kev dropped me off and I had a few prosecco's. It was lovely to see the girls and have a laugh. It was Ange, one of my good friends, 50th birthday in October. We had hoped we would all be going to Spain, however, this wasn't looking likely, so we booked a lodge with a hot tub for a weekend for us all in September and we chatted about what we would do there. It was lovely having things to look forward to. I only stayed a couple of hours as was worried about Niamh.

27/7/2020 – 29/7/2020 DAYS 151-153

Niamh was well again, and we were making the most of it before her new chemo's on Thursday. We went for a little lunch out on Monday which felt like such a treat after all this time! On Tuesday Pauline, the girls cheer coach, said she would do a little session if Niamh felt up to it -which she did and loved. Terry finished his bike ride today 4009 miles, just before Issy's birthday and over 2 months earlier than the original date he had set of 28th September, his birthday! He raised an amazing £1000 for the Children's Cancer North charity under 'Niamh's Team'.

30/7/2020 DAY 154

Today Niamh was to get her first dose of Cytarabine and another new chemo Cyclophosphamide. With us having had all the training the week before, we both thought we were prepared for what was going to happen, but it wasn't to be the case. Niamh had her counts done and she was neutropenic at 0.14 this needed to be over 0.75 her platelets were also low at 77 and hb at 99 these were boarder-line. If her platelets went lower than 70, she would need platelet transfusion and if hb went lower than 90 she would need a blood transfusion. Another week to wait! Niamh was very disappointed and got upset. Imagine being disappointed NOT to have chemo!

31/7/2020 – 2/8/2020 DAYS 155-157

It was Issy's birthday weekend a big 14. Her birthday was the Saturday, and the weather was good, so family came and seen her on and off throughout the day in the back garden. We all had a lovely day, and, on reflection, we were all quite pleased Niamh's chemo had been delayed! We put the tent up in the garden and allowed Issy to have a friend sleep over in it. Not quite the celebration Issy was used to, but we needed to be so careful with Niamh and she understood that, especially now, with Niamh being neutropenic as that means she had no resistance at all and could pick up an infection very easily.

3/8/2020 – 5/8/2020 DAYS 158-160

The 4th was a momentous day for me I finally got to the hairdressers after all these months. I felt like I had aged 10 years in this past six months! Kev's brother Paul, who lives in Wales, also came to visit and it was lovely to see him.

6/8/2020 DAY 161

We weren't getting our hopes up today! We decided to do a list of positives and negatives just in case Niamh's bloods weren't up. However, we were to be amazed, its great what your blood can do in a week when left alone without chemo. Niamh's neutrophils were 1.04, platelets 118, and hb 106! We could go ahead! Niamh got her wiggly put in and we started the first of our 2 new chemo's Cyclophosphamide. This chemo is known to really irritate the bladder so needs to be given very slowly with lots of fluid. I mean LOTS of fluid she was given bags of saline for 3 and a half hours after having the chemo. It was today that I met another lady, Claire, and her remarkable little boy, Jojo. Jojo was 6 and also having the same treatment as Niamh. However, although Jojo has ALL the same as Niamh, he has a rarer type that needs more treatment, so he was still in his induction phase but already getting this chemo that Niamh was having in delayed intensification. Claire was also giving Cytarabine at home for the next few days, she had already done this so was able to give me a little pep talk to build my confidence and put my mind at rest. These parents will always amaze me as they don't know how much the little things help. It certainly passed the long day having a chat and Jojo made us all laugh telling us about 'black holes.' I never knew there was so much information about them! Niamh was given her first dose of Cytarabine from me, with Jagoda's watchful eye and said I could change the time by an hour each day if needed as it was now 6pm. A late night by the time we arrived home and got Niamh settled. She was a bit worried about having her wiggly in again as it had been so long since she had it in at home.

7/8/2020 – 9/8/2020 DAYS 162-164

Kev and I made a good team and giving the Cytarabine went well. Niamh was quite sickly for the first 2 days and washed out but after that picked up. She spent most of Friday and Saturday asleep on the sofa. She was very worried about me taking the wiggly out. This was the worst thing about the process! On the last day I was to remove the needle from the chest, this is something that couldn't be practised first. It was fine and she even said I was better than the nurses.... although she now denies saying that! We went for an ice cream at the beach after we had done the last dose as a little treat for us all. However, in typical Niamh style she ordered an ice cream that she would normally love and when she tasted it, she no longer liked it. Therefore, Kev had to eat 2! We found this with lots of foods, tastes would change very quickly due to the chemo.

10/8/2020 – 12/8/2020 DAYS 165-167

Things were slowly getting back to normal. My boss and work colleague came over into the back garden, as weather was still good to do a welfare visit. It was lovely to see them and although I knew that I needed to be with Niamh at this time I was desperate to get back to work and do what I loved doing. I was still working on my MSc and the end of the week was my hand in date for my research proposal. We also had a leak in the house, so a surveyor came out to assess it, thankfully it wasn't serious. Another nice day and my friend Sarah brought over her little Pomeranian doggy, who Niamh loved. She promised when Niamh was feeling better, they would take Oreo out for walks together.

13/8/2020 DAY 168

Hospital day! It came around so fast! We had an early appointment today at 9.15 and we were in the quickest we had ever been so far. We just needed to get wiggly in and first dose of Cytarabine. This weekend would be a bit different as it would be done on a morning rather than teatime. Claire and Jojo were there again and having the same treatment. We chatted about how the last week had been and it made us feel better to know that both children had similar effects the first couple of days. It was definitely reassuring when you had someone to discuss things with, especially when they were going through the same as yourself. We were home before lunch, Kev and Issy couldn't believe it.

14/8/2020 – 16/8/2020 DAYS 169-171

Because we missed a week with Niamh's blood counts being low, we were a week behind where we thought we would be in the treatment schedule. It had been Kev's sister's birthday on the 12th, so he had decided to take his dad to Fort William to see her and climb Ben Nevis. That meant it was up to Issy and I to give Cytarabine. Issy as always was a great help and not particularly phased by doing it, although getting her out of bed for 10 o'clock was a challenge! I also handed in my last piece of MSc work for second year. I was quite proud of myself completing it with everything going on. It was my cousins 30th birthday on Saturday so we had a little socially distanced family party in her back garden. Issy had been at cheer for a few hours too but of course Niamh wasn't able to go as she had her wiggly in. She was much better in herself this weekend, nonetheless, still stressed out about me taking wiggly out again and this time I was nowhere near as good as HER nurses! It was this weekend I noticed Niamh's little wispy bits of hair had gone she was now 'shiny bald'.

17/8/2020 DAY 172

I've joined a gym, some time out for me! I have never really liked a gym but thought going to classes would make me feel better and it definitely did! Niamh was on great form today and she asked if we could go and get her new school shoes. I had ordered everything else online as wasn't comfortable going shopping, but she was so excited that I decided to take her. On the way we were hit in the car by a drunk driver coming the wrong way down a one-way street…..What can I say, luck was not on my side at the moment! The damage was minimal, and Niamh and I were both fine which was the most important thing, although hours of the police and insurance company dealings ensued. Niamh was quite upset about the whole thing, and it affected me so much I think it brought everything we had been through to the forefront of my mind. I was giving my statement to the policeman in the dining room and all I could focus on was an old school photograph of Niamh with long blonde plaits in her hair. What had happened to my little girl? Would she ever be the same after this brutal treatment? Then I was annoyed with myself for being so pessimistic and defeatist. Some days emotions get the better of you and this journey is definitely a rollercoaster of emotions. I think what is surprising these feelings come unexpectedly most times and not when you are in the worst of things and working on autopilot.

18/8/2020 – 19/8/2020 DAYS 173-174

The weather was beginning to be more changeable, but Niamh was good and feeling strong, so she did some cheer warm-ups. We went out for a nice lunch with my mum and stepdad it was lovely. Niamh felt sick during the meal, went to the toilet was very sick, then came back and finished her meal. That's chemo after affects for you!

20/8/2020 DAY 175

So back to RVI and back to being neutropenic and her hb and platelets very low. She needed a blood transfusion. For Niamh the worst thing! She hated seeing the blood go in and the nurses gave her a bag to put over the blood so she wouldn't have to look at it. However, Evie was there today so Niamh and her were able to have a little chat as she was also getting blood. Jojo was also there, and he was needing blood and platelets his platelet level was 1! These kids were able to run on absolutely nothing, they all amazed me every day. It is a long day when they have blood because they normally have to wait for the blood as supplies are short. It is so important to donate if you can! This blood literally saves leukaemia patients lives. It takes 3hrs for the transfusion to go through and then we wait 1hr after it is completed, to ensure there is no reaction.

I had 'bums and tums' booked at the gym for 6 o'clock, which I missed!

Niamh had started to get a rash over her face, Jagoda told me it was a chemo rash and usually it was very dry, so to put emollient creams on.

21/8/2020 – 23/8/2020 DAYS 176-178

Our friend has a boat on Lake Windermere, and they had invited us over to see them. With Niamh just having a transfusion the day before we were a bit worried, but she felt really good in herself and was excited to go. I had mentioned to Jagoda the day before and she said we should go. She gave me a letter to take with us just in case we had to go to the local hospital. We had a lovely weekend despite the rainy weather. Niamh was well in herself and loved doing normal things again.

Two things stick in my mind from today. We went to a little park and a girl of about 9 or 10 came up to Niamh and said to her mum, 'Is it a girl or a boy?' This upset me so much not because she had asked the question but that she had referred to my beautiful little girl as an 'it'. I had many a tear over that statement. I wouldn't care if she had asked, Niamh would have clearly explained why she had no hair.

The other thing that happened is Niamh tripped over whilst walking, her knee swelled so much and she had a huge bruise (haematoma) on it, again making me realise how fragile she was.

24/8/2020 – 26/8/2020 DAYS 179-181

On Monday, my step mum's sister-in-law, Kirsty invited us over to her house in Newcastle. Our girls are close and would normally spend the summer together in Spain. 'Grandma Wendy' was there too, and it was so lovely to see them. Kirsty had made us a Spanish themed lunch to pretend we were in Spain, where we all would have loved to be.

On Tuesday Kev and I had a meeting with Niamh's head mistress and discussed things we felt Niamh would need in place for her return to school. We had to sign and fill out lots of forms for the administration of medication, such as anti-sickness which she still required to have quite often. We also expressed our concerns about how other children would react to her appearance. Due to Covid risk assessments, Niamh's class would be in their own bubble. The class had been given information about Niamh's illness when she was first diagnosed. This made us all feel more confident and better prepared for Niamh going back to school. Kev decided at this time, as if we didn't have enough on, he was going to apply for another job in a different police force. Still a local force but the job would be a promotion to chief inspector, I was worried he wouldn't enjoy it as much as being frontline, but he was very keen to do it and I would never stand in his way. He threw all his time and effort into preparing for his interview, but maintenance was coming, and we were promised big things!

LONG-TERM MAINTENANCE

27/8/2020 DAY 182

Back at hospital, and the day we go into 'maintenance'. Again, it was a defining day for Niamh as the doctors and nurses talk of this 'maintenance' as getting your life back and returning to normality. Just in case it didn't happen I prepared Niamh that it may not happen if her bloods were not right just like last time. We had booked a little cottage for the weekend to celebrate 'maintenance' however, when we booked it, we thought we would be a week ahead into this cycle. Niamh scraped through with her neutrophils being 0.1 over what they needed to be, but we could start!! Woohoo we were in maintenance. This felt like such an achievement, and we were on a high. Although, this was to be short lived when we were told she was going straight back onto steroids and Vincristine plus another 2 oral chemotherapies and then the following week she would be back for a magic sleep. This didn't really feel like the 'maintenance' we had been sold. However, Evie was there which helped, and she loved feeling Niamh's soft head with her being shiny bald. We got told off for not socially distancing!

28/8/2020 – 31/8/2020 DAYS 183-186

The weather was typically British and rained and rained. Our friends were camping on the site where the cottage was. They demonstrated unbelievable dedication to camp in that weather! We all made the best of it and had a lovely time. The kids all played together and although Niamh was feeling very low being on steroids again, she was so pleased to be able to play with other kids. One day they were all playing and running around when some other children from the site joined in. A little girl said to her, 'Have you got cancer?' One of Niamh's friends, Charlotte, got really upset by her saying this, as did Niamh! I just wanted to take her away, she was so defined by her loss of hair although apart from this she looked really well. I had a chat with Niamh about what people say and that sometimes they don't understand so we must explain things to them. She told me she was happy to tell anyone about what she was going through.

By now Niamh was sick of even trying to bother with wigs and had completely embraced her baldness. She wore beautiful little hair bands, and we loved her 'baldy' head as we called it.

1/9/2020 DAY 187

Last day before school. Niamh had finished her steroids as it was a five-day course in 'maintenance'. I nearly said only 5 days – but there is no 'only' with steroids! Niamh was excited about school she felt well in herself, although a bit apprehensive made more so by the comments from the few children we had bumped into. I must admit I was a bit anxious about her going back. We had kept her safe and secure for so long and I was worried if someone did say something to upset her at school, I wouldn't be there. I reminded Niamh about our previous chat and what to say and how to deal with any questions. By this point she knew the names of all her medications and what they were for, she would often give Kev a lesson in this.

2/9/2020 DAY 188

First day back at school. Brought memories of me asking the nurse, in the middle of the night, when Niamh would get back…..well she was right 6 MONTHS!! I really feel if COVID hadn't been about Niamh would have been back much sooner but, this was the way of the world at the moment. We were all excited for her going back and she was really brave going in. Everything was very different children and parents couldn't meet before going into class. This unnerved Niamh slightly as I think it would have given her more confidence for them to see her with no hair and just be excited to have her back. I would have liked to speak to the teachers, but I couldn't, it made me feel out of control.

I felt overwhelmed when I got back in the car wondering- Had I done the right thing? Would she be ok? What if she picked something up from school or contracted Covid? I felt lost without her. But I reminded myself this was the best thing for her and that's what I needed to concentrate on…it wasn't easy! Niamh came out of school and was on a high. I was so pleased about making the decision I had made I hadn't seen her like this in months. How much better you feel when your mind is taken off something and you have time spent with friends.

3/9/2020 DAY 189

Our first week off from RVI on a Thursday. This was to be a regular occurrence with 'maintenance' and we loved it. Niamh, was of course, at school. I did a gym class and spent a bit of time with Issy as she wasn't due back until the next day. Kev was busy preparing for his interview which was to be on 15th September, and it felt like all his time was taken up doing this. I did have to remind him that he said it wouldn't be like that but as with everything he does he gives it 110%.

4/9/2020 – 6/9/2020 DAYS 190-192

I finally felt like life was getting back to some normality. Both girls were at school, Kev was back at work, and I would be returning to work the following week. Cheerleading started again the following Saturday and both girls were desperate to go and see their 'cheer friends.' Niamh went to a party on Saturday afternoon after cheer. Issy had her first sleepover and I met up with all the girls on Sunday night when Ange cooked us an amazing meal. It felt so good to be just doing ordinary things and time with friends was always a tonic.

7/9/2020/- 9/9/2020 DAYS 193-195

On Monday I went to see my bosses about my return to work. They did not want me to have patient contact as felt it was still too dangerous as I worked in a high-risk area where we would be exposed to COVID regularly. I would be working in the office and at home when I was able to get home working equipment.

I did a few gym classes and Kev, and I went over to our friends for tea on Tuesday. It felt fantastic to have a bit of time on my own and time with Kev. The girls were both loving being back at school and seeing their friends. It was now that it was necessary for Niamh to have a COVID swab prior to theatre. She was still allowed to go to school in between having this, which we were pleased about, given that she would be missing so much time already with hospital days.

10/9/2020 DAY 196

Another trip to the RVI and another theatre day for us. Niamh was maintaining her bloods which they were really pleased about as she was on 100% doses of 6mp and Methotrexate. Niamh's chemo rash had tracked up a bit close to her eye. I asked again about it, but they told me not to worry. Niamh was fantastic, she amazed me how she took it all in her stride. She laughed and joked as we walked her to theatre, once in the room she pulled over her eye mask which she always wore and said 'Goodnight'. How having a general anaesthetic can come second nature to a child was just so wrong but she managed it fantastically. Luckily it wasn't too long a wait today. The first question on arrival was always, 'How many are on the list?' Then we would scan the room to see what ages people were, as the youngest always went first. The theatre list itself didn't start until 1pm but often it was after 2pm when they started calling them down and that was the worst thing the waiting and the starving! Anyway, today wasn't too bad and Niamh went to theatre just after 3.30. I must say at this time the theatre staff in the children's theatre are absolutely astounding. Sharon on reception would always make Niamh feel at ease and chat with her, the porters would make a fuss of her and be there when she woke to take us back to the ward telling her silly jokes and making her laugh. When I went to collect her, she was busy talking to the nurse, who was looking after her, telling her everything she had to eat when she went back to the ward, no more crying waiting for me to come! We got back to the ward she jumped off the trolley and onto a chair (you would not have thought she had just had a big needle into her back). We had to wait an hour when she got back to the ward after theatre, but then we were good to go home.

Evie was an inpatient on ward 4 she had spiked a temp and was in hospital having intravenous antibiotics. Niamh was upset we didn't see her, so we dropped a little card off at the entrance to the ward for her.

11/9/2020 – 13/9/2020 DAYS 197-199

Again, some lovely days. Doing normal and routine things. Then, for no reason at all and completely out of the blue Niamh woke up and was in agony with her back, she couldn't even walk downstairs and had to go on her bum. I gave her some pain killers and got her comfy on the sofa with her iPad, cushions and a hot water bottle. When I came back, she was doing her English homework on her iPad. I phoned the school and said she was in pain, and I wasn't sure if she would make it in today. After she had finished her homework, she said she felt she should try and get dressed and go into school as the pain killers had helped. She went in at 9,30 only missing 45 minutes of school! She also got 'worker of the week'. However, school was more than enough for her as she was shattered when she got in and couldn't make cheer which she was upset about.

My aunty had booked us an afternoon tea it was lovely to see her and have time to chat.

A close friend from my school days wanted to organise an event that would give Niamh something to look forward to but also raise money for 'Niamh's Team'. She arranged a committee meeting with family and friends to plan for a 'Funday'. A date was decided for September 2021, in the hope that Covid restrictions would be finished by then. A WhatsApp group was established to organise the event. The WhatsApp was also a good way to keep everyone in the loop about how Niamh was doing.

A new ruling was also introduced today- due to covid, groups of 6 were only allowed in any scenario, we had booked the lodge for 8 of us for Ange's big 50th in just 2 weeks time……arghhh!

14/9/2020 - 17/9/2020 DAYS 200-203

I was back at work, Kev went for his interview. Unfortunately, after all that time spent preparing for his interview, he did not get the job. Previously this would have devastated him however, although very disappointed, he had much greater concerns now than a failed interview. We went out for a lovely meal together, I really felt we had turned a corner. We had started to leave Niamh with grandparents babysitting again and it was doing us all good. No hospital visits this week. I was enjoying the gym it was nice to have some 'me' time and join a class. It did feel strange after all this time going out and doing normal things. Niamh did a full week back at school. I was extremely proud of her, not that it phased her at all. She took it all in her stride. She was definitely getting back to herself although that's not to say we didn't have our hard days. She would get upset about how she looked (i.e. if her chemo rash flared up all over her beautiful face or her hair which was just starting to grow became unruly).

18/9/2020 DAY 204

Kev went away this morning to Gdansk in Poland, a little jolly with his friends. After Niamh finished school, we went and said thank you to the staff in our local Tesco who had helped us so much during lockdown. We took a card and some flowers for the manager. They completely overwhelmed us by giving Niamh a collection the staff had donated to buy herself something, we were meant to be thanking them! Girls both went to cheer and enjoyed it. When Niamh came home, she complained about feeling itchy on her back she had a small area of dry skin which looked like eczema, it looked a bit like the rash she had on her face so I wondered again if it might be caused by chemo, but I wasn't too worried as she was so well in herself.

Sadly, we heard today that Evie had been admitted to hospital again with yet another temp. she was having such a hard time of it, bouncing back and forwards to hospital. I worried about Tina also they had so far to travel to hospital as they lived even further away than us.

19/9/20 DAY 205

My mum went away this morning on a little break to Scotland. Girls went to cheer, I went to the gym after dropping them off and enjoyed a bit of time on my own, it had been a while! When I collected Niamh, the coach said she had complained of her back hurting a bit when she was stunting. I brought her home and she was fine, she played on the trampoline and then came with me to collect Issy. The girls had their tea and as I was bathing Niamh, I noticed that she now had more areas of what I had thought was 'eczema' and it was spreading and growing bigger. I put a picture on one of the leukaemia groups I had joined. Immediately a parent messaged me to say she thought it was shingles and I needed to go straight to hospital with Niamh…..NO!!! I rung the ward and the Dr asked for me to send a photo. On receiving it she said she was concerned and needed to see Niamh. Kev was away, my mum was away…typical! Issy rang one of her friends and her mum kindly said Issy could go and stay there. Off we went to A&E. luckily one of the nurses from the ward was working in A&E that night, so she did her port access and we had yet another Covid swab. The Dr said Niamh had to be admitted and she would need IV Aciclovir an anti viral medication, which was to be started immediately. We were taken to the ward and until we got our covid results back neither Niamh nor I were allowed to leave the room. Meals and drinks were brought to us.

Evie was also confined to a room so we were texting each other arranging to meet in the coffee room when we could. Niamh seemed well and we thought, surely, we would only be in a day or so. In fact, she was so well she had been recording TikTok's at 9pm in A&E.

20/9/2020 DAY 206

Kev was obviously passed himself being away and Niamh in hospital. I told him there was nothing he could do, but it was awful for him. Coming out in such a rush last night and trying to get Issy sorted I had left 3 vital things - Niamh's 6mp chemo, her eye mask and her sheet, a little muslin cloth she liked to put over the hospital pillow as she said it was scratchy! I phoned Terry and he said he would drop them off. I was allowed to go out and get them from him but could go nowhere else on the ward. Niamh had her 'doggy' back again, she wasn't very happy, but we still thought it wouldn't be for long. She was having lots of doses of Acyclovir and fluid continuously. She was tired today as it had been very late by the time, they got us settled into a bed on ward 4, the oncology ward, where we had been when Niamh was first diagnosed. We had a day of her snoozing on and off and watching rubbish TV together. It's a good job as we hardly got any sleep that night. Niamh went to sleep at the normal time for her about 7pm, but then the nurses were in and out giving her medicines. At 23.35 she was back up having a snack and watching her iPad! It went from bad to worse during the night. Niamh had two lines taking the medication and fluid into her port. On the line that had her medication after it had finished, they would put up a small amount of fluid 'a flush' in and they would put 10mls into the machine. After this 10mls went in, the machine would start bleeping again, repeatedly. As I still wasn't allowed to leave the room, we had to keep pressing the buzzer. Niamh was also up and down to the toilet with all the fluid she was being given. At 4am when the machine was bleeping for what felt like the 100th time (I'm sure it wasn't but with sleep deprivation it definitely felt like that!) I asked why the flush was put on for 10mls, the nurse informed me because they just set it for 10mls. I replied but then you come in and set for another 10 and another. I suggested if it could be put on 100mls but 10mls per hour then it would go in as you are setting it. She said she hadn't thought of that! I was proud of myself that I hadn't lost all my clinical abilities as a nurse.

Kev and I had booked, as a surprise, for the girls to go to Center Parcs next week, obviously with shingles we would need to cancel this. I had only been back at work a few days. I rung work and explained I hoped we would get out the next day, but they said I didn't need to worry at all. Issy was still ok at her friends and luckily her mum was more than happy to keep her that night as well. Niamh was back on fluid which meant all wee samples being saved again and measuring…my most hated job!

21/9/2020 DAY 207

We finally got Niamh's covid swab result, negative. So, we were free - sort of! Geoff came with the disappointing news that Niamh would need at least 3-5 days of Acyclovir through her port. This gave us both a shock, we weren't expecting that! Though Niamh had started to be quite sickly again and wasn't as well in herself. He said we could leave the room as it wasn't contagious to anyone else. Jagoda was off this week, which Niamh was upset about. Jojo and Claire were brought in late that night so there was a hat-trick. Another day of Niamh sleeping on and off, Kev was back tonight so Issy was going to Mel's after school for tea, then Kev would collect her. Niamh was very lethargic today and very sickly on and off. She couldn't even be bothered to go and see Evie as she didn't feel well. Her bloods found that the Acyclovir was starting to affect her kidneys and it had given her an acute kidney injury or AKI. This basically meant her kidneys weren't working as they should. Of course, they could not stop the anti virals so they gave more fluid to try and flush it out. Geoff also reduced her chemo to 50% as he was worried about the strain on her body due to the shingles.

22/9/2002 DAY 208

Tina and Evie had been moved into the 4 bedded bay. Tina wasn't very pleased at first but when they got in there were 2 other girls, Ruby aged 10 and Ari aged 3 and then Jojo was also moved there. Ruby had a very, very rare cancer 'Mesenchymal Chondrosarcoma' this type of cancer had never been seen before in a child, prior to

Ruby, and was in her scapula bone. Ari had Bilateral Wilms' tumours which is a rare kidney cancer that primarily affects children. All these cancers are classified as rare however, when you are in this world 'Rare' is the last thing they feel.

Niamh was feeling a bit better and desperate to see Evie, so we spent a bit of time in the bay too it was so lovely for the kids to be able to see one another. The teachers came around and played curling with them and Evie did a little sing song for us all. They were ordering a takeaway, but Niamh tired quickly so we went back to our side room. Kev was back too, so he came over and was allowed in for an hour but only if I left the room. I went for a little walk whilst he stayed with Niamh and played cards. It was good just to get out of the ward. Niamh became very tired again and her legs had started to swell. I informed the nurses about this, and the Dr came back in and said the kidney function had worsened again so they needed to give her a diuretic medication, Frusemide, to try and push the fluid out of her body. By now I realised these shingles were having quite serious consequences. Niamh got really tired easily on a night and she used to ring my dad on facetime on her iPad and he would read to her, she would fall asleep whilst he was reading. With the diuretic medication Niamh was up nearly every hour during the night for the toilet.

I messaged all the girls saying about the weekend we were meant to be at the lodge, 2 had said they weren't going due to the COVID rule, so it was just the 6 of us and I had been looking forward to it so much. I said that it was unlikely I would be able to make it, so if one of others wanted to go again, they could have my place.

23/9/2020 DAY 209

Kev was at work today. I told him to go to work as the staff were not keen on visitors and there was nothing more he could do being here. It was awkward as if he came, I had to leave, it was not as if I could go home and have a nice shower or anything as we lived over an hour away, it just wasn't feasible. Geoff and another Dr came this morning. They had seen an improvement in Niamh's bloods since giving the diuretic medication. Geoff said he had decided that he didn't want her to have tomorrows pulse of Vinc/Dex as he wanted to give her more time to recover and it would not matter missing a pulse. Niamh and I certainly weren't going to argue about not having steroids!! And we were to continue on only 50% of chemo at the moment until our next clinic visit. Niamh felt much better, although tired after the night's frequent toilet trips. We had a great day in the bay with the gang. They did animation, more curling, TikTok's and fashion shows. We even ordered a takeaway on the night with the others. However, Niamh became tired before it came so I took her to bed, and she had something there and went straight to sleep. I went back and had my food with the others, it was so lovely to have people to talk to it made our time in hospital so very different from our previous admittance.

24/9/2020 DAY 210

Again, Niamh continued to improve as we went for our daily visit to the bay. The nurse in charge came in and told us we were not allowed to mix and had to stay in our own room because of COVID. She also said that no more takeaways were allowed! This really upset Niamh as she was starting to not fear hospital as much and have a bit of fun. We went back to our little room, and I played with her. The teachers both came into see her and she had the opportunity to do a science experiment and play some golf. Just after lunch the nurse who had earlier told us off, now said there would be some space in the bay if we wanted to move - of course we did! Didn't think I would ever give up a side room and a bed to sleep on a chair!!

We needed to wait for the other child to leave. This seemed to take hours and we were all packed up desperate to go into the bay, then would you believe Tina came to see us at the door and told us Evie was able to go home! Anyway, we had made our decision and there was no going back now although Niamh said, 'Well, I'm not moving then!' The staff also said they hoped that we would get home the following day. We moved into the bay eventually, after teatime. Niamh and Evie had about 15 minutes together before Evie's dad came to pick them up. Jojo also went home, so there was just us and Ruby left.

25/9/2020 DAY 211

We got the green light that we could go home today. We needed prescriptions as they wanted Niamh to stay on the anti virals and they had to give her a very specific one, due to the kidney issues she had. Niamh's prescription came quite quickly so we got home for just after lunch time. We managed to squeeze in another lesson before we left, where Niamh made an exploding volcano! Ruby enjoyed watching it too and we said bye to her and her mum Sarah. I should have been going to the lodge today but knew I was exhausted, needed an early night in my own bed. Once home, Niamh and I had a lovely bath, and both had a very early night.

Kev told me I should go on Saturday as he had taken the weekend off work and wanted me to have some time away. One of the other girls was going to drive me over on the Saturday morning.

26/9/2020 – 27/9/2020 DAYS 212-213

Well, I eventually got to the lodge. I didn't think I would make it at all at some points during the week. I was so pleased I had, it was lovely to see all the girls, be there for Ange's birthday and just have a giggle and relax. We had a meal booked for the Saturday, late afternoon, and then went to a bar for a few drinks. Although it was a very surreal experience! People weren't allowed to leave their seats but be served at the table. We had to wear masks to walk in and out of anywhere and to go to the toilet! The world was a very different place since COVID. It was worth it though just to be away and have a laugh with the girls. Niamh was of course not best pleased I was leaving her but Kev and Issy made a fuss and had a takeaway night. I think she spent most of the weekend on facetime to Erin, catching up on all that she had missed the previous week at school!

28/9/2020 – 30/9/2020 DAYS 214-216

Niamh was amazing to say what she had went through only the week before and she wanted to go back to school on Monday. It was also Grandad's birthday, so we made him a nice tea to celebrate. The bike ride that was meant to finish today seemed long ago now. We should have been in Center Parcs so we decided to take the girls for a nice day out and keep them off school for one day. We went to a local theme park. We had a lovely day, and it was great having some time together in a fun environment. The theme park wasn't busy, and the girls loved going on some of the bigger rides that Niamh was now tall enough for and went on again and again. We went to a little park area and there were two other kids playing. One said to Niamh, 'why have you got a boy's hairstyle?' Niamh came over a bit quiet but didn't get upset. I explained again that some children don't understand and ask things when they maybe shouldn't.

Niamh was on lots of medications as the anti virals needed taking 5 times a day, and her rash was still very widespread and angry. We were back for an unplanned trip to the hospital on Thursday as they wanted to review her.

1/10/2020 DAY 217

Another RVI visit. Her bloods weren't any better so continuing with 50% chemo still. Evie was there too, and we decided that we would go for a Costa with the girls after we had finished as it was hopefully going to be a quick day for us both. Niamh's shingle rash was still really bad, and the Dr was concerned so gave yet another week of antivirals. They added on her kidney function with her bloods because of all the problems we had in hospital, Jagoda was back and thought it best to get it checked, which I agreed. After we finished, we went with Evie to Costa the girls had a vanilla frappe each and it was lovely to sit and have a chat together. The girls loved it, and we kept finding more and more that they had in common. Evie loved to feel Niamh's little baldie head.

2/10/2020 – 7/10/2020 DAYS 218-223

A very uneventful week thankfully. We were all getting back into the routine of school and work and loving every minute of the monotony of it! The RVI had told me the whole family, including Niamh, had to get the flu vaccine. Niamh wasn't very happy about this and Issy even less so. Issy went on and on about being scared about having it! I had mine at work, but Kev and the girls had to have theirs at the GPs. You would have thought I was asking for the world off the GP for this as it was a mission to get them to agree to it! In the end I had to go into the GP surgery and appeal to the receptionist's better nature and explain how important it was they had them.

8/10/2020 DAY 224

Back to Newcastle! Niamh's blood counts had now all dropped further. She was neutropenic and borderline to need blood and platelets. They decided to hold off blood and platelets for now but to also put a complete stop on chemotherapy. This concerned me obviously it was the first time this had happened to Niamh. It seemed to be a continuation of the shingles. Evie was having a platelet transfusion, so we waited for her to finish then went for our little Costa date. This was becoming a regular occurrence and the girls loved it. It was also nice for Tina and I to chat. We also met Lacey and her mum, Leah, whilst waiting for Evie to finish. Lacey had not long been diagnosed and was very nervous about the finger prick, so Niamh was chatting to her about it. Lacey was only 3 and very timid and nervous of what was going on, she listened to Niamh quietly.

9/10/2020 DAY 225

Things definitely felt like they were getting back to normal. The girls were back at cheer on a Friday and Saturday, I was getting to the gym and working. My mum had booked the girls into a Ninja Park on Sunday, and they couldn't wait to try that. Niamh was so much stronger. Unfortunately, Tina text late on to say Evie had been admitted again.

10/10/2020 – 11/10/2020 DAYS 226-227

The girls went to cheer this morning and I went out for brekky with one of my friends, Allison. Ruby, her daughter, goes to cheer with the girls, and they couldn't have been any more helpful to us throughout the time Niamh was ill. Sending little boxes of her favourite sweets, bringing their dog 'Milo,' whom Niamh loved, over to see her. After breakfast Ali told me that they would bring Niamh home as they would take Milo to get her from cheer - she would love this. When Niamh got home, she was on cloud 9 as Milo had sat on her knee in the back of the car. I went and picked Issy up and I was just getting tea ready when Niamh said she didn't feel well. I did her temperature and sure enough 38.1!! I called the hospital as per procedure and, not surprisingly, was told I had to get there within an hour! Off we went again, Niamh perked up as we neared the hospital as I had been allowed to give her Calpol before leaving home, so she had no spike in temperature and felt better! The usual ensued accessed port, intravenous antibiotics given, bloods taken and of course the dreaded COVID test done. I was concerned as she had been neutropenic on Thursday that this could be sepsis. Niamh was quite sick when they accessed her port and the Dr said she was worried she had a port infection - I didn't think so I just thought she was getting herself in a bit of a state because of her port being accessed. Always on a weekend! However, Niamh wasn't too bothered and was in some ways excited she would see Evie! We were put into a side room awaiting covid test result and by the time we got to the ward it was late and we were both shattered. Another Dr came around in the middle of the night as she said she wanted to review Niamh due to her port infection. I told her I didn't think it was that, but she said she wanted to be cautious so continuing with a very high dose antibiotic. The next morning Geoff was the consultant on call, which was lucky, he agreed with me about port infection and said he didn't think she had one and unbelievably her neutrophils had come up to normal range since Thursday. Niamh was actually doing a dancing TikTok when he came into the room, so he said with her looking very well she could be discharged with oral antibiotics straight away! How fantastic when your own consultant is on, what a difference! He also said the covid swab was back and negative so Niamh could go and see Evie! We had to wait a few hours for Niamh to get her antibiotics to take home, so we went and sat with Evie and the girls played. We eventually got home about 6pm and my mum had made us a Sunday dinner which we enjoyed and then went to bed.

12/10/2020 – 18/10/2020 DAYS 228-234

Lots of extra medication for Niamh to take with the antibiotics, from the hospital. Niamh insisted she wanted to go straight back to school on Monday. I went back to work and finally got a home laptop in case I needed to be at home again or to take with me to hospital so I could still work. On Wednesday I had to ring and ensure Niamh's blood culture hadn't grown anything because, if it had, we would have had to return to hospital for more antibiotics. It hadn't, so thankfully we were allowed to stop the other medications she was on.

19/10/2020 – 21/10/2020 DAYS 235-237

Kev and Issy went for their flu jabs. Niamh was not allowed hers until her counts were stable. Issy whinged about it so much saying she didn't dare have it, but then came back saying she didn't even feel it!

22/10/2020 DAY 238

RVI day again and Niamh's counts had improved slightly for her hb and platelets however she was still neutropenic. They made the decision that she could have Vincristine and Dexamethasone as they are not count dependent, she was still not allowed any oral chemotherapies though, including her 6mp and Methotrexate, this was to be her 4th week of chemo on hold. Niamh had developed a rash all over her face which was now getting worse. They termed this a 'chemo rash' and agreed it was getting worse but decided to wait and see if it improved when she went back onto chemo.

24/10/2020 – 25/10/2020 DAYS 239-240

Niamh was sad again all weekend. She fell asleep on Friday after school but insisted she wanted to go to cheer, for her to be sent home again by the coach half hour later. She didn't make it the next morning either as she was worn out. Kev's dad was going to Scotland on Sunday to see Jan, so he asked if Issy wanted to go with him. She jumped at the chance to see her aunty and when Niamh was on steroids the house wasn't much fun! All Niamh wanted to eat at this time was McDonalds. Don't judge me but she had one 3 days running - not something I would ever normally do but if you have a child on high doses of steroids you will do anything to make them feel a bit better and feed their cravings.

26/10/2020 – 28/10/2020 DAYS 241-243

We arranged some nice things to do. Kev and I had the week off and girls were off school. With Issy away we booked to take Niamh to the cinema, it was lovely getting back to do normal things. Niamh also went to a little gymnastic camp and loved it. We bought a pumpkin ready for Halloween and Niamh and Kev spent time carving it out. We were going away at the weekend to a caravan which a lovely family at the hospital kindly rent out to families on treatment. Issy came back on Wednesday and Niamh was so pleased to see her, as she was now off steroids, and they hadn't spent hardly any time apart for the past 6 months.

29/10/2020 DAY 244

Tonight, was extremely hard Niamh was really upset as Evie had been admitted to hospital again. She was very poorly this time. Evie had been selected to go on 'Operation Ouch' which she had delighted in telling Niamh about last Thursday, she was so excited about it. Some videoing had been done today in hospital and Evie had not been able to interact as she was feeling so poorly. Niamh knew how excited Evie was about it and got really concerned about how poorly she was. Naively, this was something up until now I had not considered her seeing her friends becoming very poorly. I chatted with her for a long time about when she was in hospital and how ill she was with the Aciclovir and it was Evie's medicines making her feel this way, she sobbed for a very long time.

30/10/2020 – 1/11/2020 DAYS 245-247

We had a lovely weekend away together although the weather was absolutely awful! It rained most of the weekend, but we had taken our bikes and were determined to get out. We even had a couple of hours walking along Blackpool promenade. We all went swimming in the pool and the girls loved it, we played games and just had a great time being together. We went out for a meal on our last night and as we came out of the restaurant a little girl followed us out, and asked me, 'why doesn't your little girl have any hair?' She asked in a lovely way, and I explained to her that Niamh needs special medicine as she is poorly, and that medicine makes her lose her hair. I told her that Niamh used to have long hair just like her and it would grow back. Children are inquisitive and will be interested it's all about how they ask, and Niamh noticed this too. She said to me that was nice how that girl asked about my hair.

2/11/2020 – 4/11/2020 DAYS 248-250

Back to work and girls back at school. Apart from Niamh on this chemo break, which was worrying me, she was looking so healthy at the minute; her strength was building back up and she was back at gymnastics and cheerleading and loving every minute. At this time, I felt like I had lost all sense of my own identity. I think I felt that we had been on this whirlwind journey where our only focus was Niamh, mixed in with COVID-19 hitting and being in complete isolation. Now things were opening back up and Kev was keen for us to go away together for a night, although, I felt like all I could concentrate on was Niamh. I'm unsure if this makes sense but I just didn't feel like me anymore. The world went back into a national lockdown again! Schools were to stay open but everything else would close. This time it was allowed for Grandparents to be in a 'family bubble' if needed for childcare, my mum had been helping quite a bit getting Niamh from school and I was glad it could continue, if only selfishly so we could see her.

5/11/2020 DAY 251

Back to RVI and Niamh's bloods had improved…woohoo!! Never thought I'd say that to be back on chemo! Niamh's facial rash had got even worse and when we got to the hospital they also agreed. We saw Geoff and he said he was still reluctant to refer to dermatology but decided to start her on Hydrocortisone steroid cream. We had a nice little Costa with Evie again.

6/11/2020 – 10/11/2020 DAYS 252-256

School was going well for the girls. Kev and I were both busy at work. Now Niamh was back on all oral chemo's again we had to get back into our routine of the starving and administering the tablets after starving.

11/11/20 DAY 257

Today was my mum's birthday. Niamh also had her flu jab as she was now eventually allowed as no longer neutropenic. This was of no concern to Niamh of course with all she had been through. We went to see Mum after Niamh had finished school, took her pressies and had some cake. I had booked to take my mum away to Edinburgh for the night but obviously this was cancelled with us being back in lockdown.

12/11/2020 – 15/11/2020 DAYS 258-261

Niamh and Grandad often played schools and it became Niamh's favourite thing to do. Her grandad was called Oscar and Niamh was Mrs O'Connor she spent hours sorting out work for him and then giving him work in class and even homework! This weekend was spent playing schools.

16/11/2020 – 18/11/2020 DAYS 262-264

My first day back at work ringing patients and not in the office - I absolutely loved it!! We had parents evening for Niamh online on Wednesday, Mrs O'Connor (the real one) said that Niamh was not behind even from the time she had missed, she said her reading had improved. Probably from all the reading in the early days with her papa and nanny over facetime. Mrs O'Connor referred to Niamh as a 'real life superhero' she certainly was in our eyes!

19/11/2020 DAY 265

Hospital day. Start of cycle 2 maintenance. Vinc and Dex again- these 4 weeks came around so quick. Bloods were still good Niamh's rash not so good! I spoke to Jagoda about it and then we saw Geoff. Jagoda felt we needed a referral to dermatology, and she told Geoff this. Evie had been admitted to the ward again, so we did not get to see her today. There were no Christmas decorations on the ward as everything had been stopped due to covid.

Both Lacey, Reuben and Perrie were all there today. Craig was telling me how Reuben had also had shingles just upon going into maintenance. However, he had a very mild attack and just needed oral anti virals this demonstrates how different viruses have such contrasting symptoms on individual children. Craig told me this as he was rushing out of the ward as he now managed to get the earliest appointment every Thursday and was always finished before us all. Lacey and her mum Leah often brought arts and crafts with them, and Lacey and Niamh would do these together, socially distanced of course!

20/11/2020 – 22/11/2020 DAYS 266-268

We could book up our Christmas Center Parcs break activities so we enjoyed doing this over the weekend, although we were not convinced, we were going to be able to get there as it hadn't been confirmed how long this lockdown would last. Clic Sargeant now known as 'Young lives v cancer' the charity that gives support to young people with cancer and their families, had asked any children if they would sing a Christmas carol to try and raise money for the charity. Niamh always keen to help, recorded 'Away in a Manger' which was put on their charity video. Of course, the steroids kicked in again and Niamh did not want me to leave her side. Cheer was again cancelled due to lockdown, but I don't think Niamh would have made it as she felt so grotty with the Dex.

23/11/2020 – 27/11/2020 DAYS 269-273

The steroids seemed to get worse every course she had. This time I have felt like I have a newborn, not sleeping; a needy toddler, who wants to be by your side even coming to the toilet with you; and a hormonal teenager all put together. We put up all our Christmas lights very early for us as nothing else to do with lockdown and it felt nice and Christmassy. We continued getting photos from people doing the Shave4Niamh and donations were still coming in.

28/11/2020 – 29/11/2020 DAYS 274-276

In one of their school days Niamh and Grandad had written a poem about what it has been like being diagnosed with leukaemia.

Leukaemia you're breaking my heart,
Leukaemia you have torn my world apart.
Hello leukaemia what does this mean?
2 years of treatment to be clean.
I've got to listen to the Drs advice,
and some of the treatment won't be nice!
The chemo means I have lost my hair,
But if it makes me better, I don't care!
I'm not a Dr but I've made a conclusion
That I feel much better after a blood transfusion.
The steroids are awful, they make me feel mad,
And sometimes I shout at my Mum and my Dad.
But they understand it's not really me
And I'm really sorry but it's the steroids you see!
It's been 9 months now and everyone has been so kind,
And all the gifts I have been sent have blown my mind.
Geoff the consultant and all his staff
Have been so brilliant and made me laugh
I don't want this to end by being a moaner
So let's all stay safe and put an end to Corona!

I also seen a message on one of the leukaemia 'help' groups today that said as soon as children went into maintenance, they were allowed to get a puppy. As you know Niamh was absolutely desperate for a puppy. I told Kev what I had seen and that was it, he was searching for puppies. I said I felt like I needed to speak with Geoff and Jagoda about it as previously they had been so against new pets. This did not deter Kev and he was busy looking on Pets4homes.

We knew exactly what Niamh wanted as she had researched it all herself. She wanted a white maltipoo, it was to be a boy and called 'Teddy'. The prices of puppies had tripled since lockdown! We found exactly what we wanted close by, and she had 2 boys one white and one slate grey. Kev said he liked the slate grey, but I said we had to get the white one. He made an appointment for us to go and see them the next day whilst the girls were at school. I still hadn't spoken to the hospital, however, Niamh was in theatre the following Thursday, so it was perfect timing to discuss it with them.

30/11/2020 – 2/12/2020 DAYS 277-279

We went to see the baby maltipoos today, I was not a dog fan at all and wasn't convinced it was going to be for us. But when we went and met them, I was so excited that we might be able to do this as a huge surprise for the girls! Kev asked to see the slate grey and I said the white. They were both absolutely tiny we were only able to see them outside due to COVID. Kev held the grey and me the white. The white one laid in my hands and went to sleep he was so content. The lady was very understanding that we couldn't say for definite if we could have one until Thursday, and she said if we were able to tell her which one, we would definitely want, she wouldn't allow anyone else to see him. She said she thought Kev would win! On the way home I said that we had to go for the white, Kev joked and said the grey would match our furniture better!! I rung the lady and told her the white and we would be in touch on Thursday.

Niamh also had her COVID swab today ahead of theatre on Thursday.

I was able to work the next 2 days, but Niamh was now not allowed in school and had to isolate after her COVID negative swab and prior to theatre. Kev continued to look at Pets4homes and various other maltipoos for sale, I told him if we were allowed, we were getting the white one, which we had already seen.

3/12/2020 DAY 280

Niamh was in theatre another long, long day. Thankfully Evie and Ruby were there and helped to keep us entertained even though Niamh was hangry!! Niamh didn't go to theatre until 4pm after being starved from 7am! Luckily, I was able to grab Jagoda and then Geoff to ask whether a dog was at all possible. The answer was

YES!! Obviously, they emphasised how clean we would have to be and follow the best hygiene practices we could. This was a given for us anyway. As soon as Niamh went down to theatre, I phoned Kev, and he contacted the breeder and paid a deposit for the white maltipoo – Teddy! Niamh came round so quickly after the anaesthetic when I went to theatre, she was teaching the recovery nurse that everyone's fist in a ball is the same size as their heart! As we came back on the theatre bed, Evie was just going as she had been waiting for a blood transfusion. The girls said a goodbye to each other whilst Niamh was still on her theatre trolley. She then ate all her packed lunch, and we could go home after an hour of being back from theatre.

4/12/2020 – 6/12/2020 DAYS 280-282

Niamh woke up in lots of pain, she couldn't even walk down the stairs. I brought her down and gave her some morphine, which she hadn't needed to have for ages. I settled her on the sofa and thought she would put some TV on whilst I got her oral chemo and made Issy's brekky. When I went in, she was sat on the sofa doing her Reading Plus work - she said, 'Well I need to do my work to keep up!' Issy went off to school and after about 40 mins Niamh said,' I need to try and get my uniform on and go into school.' How determined is that!

I was on a course online all weekend, so the girls went to my mums on Saturday and stayed overnight.

7/12/2020 – 13/12/2020 DAYS 283-289

Niamh got her school picture during the week. She was a little baldie on it but looked so gorgeous we had to buy it for our memories. A week of working without little else to do again with being in lockdown. I was just so pleased the girls had some normality with school. There was talk that the schools could get shut again ……surely that couldn't happen! Kev and I were so excited about the girls getting Teddy at Christmas. We told my mum and stepdad during the week as Teddy would have to go to their house, so we needed to make sure it was okay with them. My mum wasn't an animal lover at all, but they said, 'Yes'. They both couldn't believe how excited we were about it, but I was so excited for the girls and especially Niamh I knew she wouldn't be able to believe it.

14/12/2020 – 16/12/2020 DAYS 290-292

Center Parcs was cancelled - Again! The government issued another announcement advising that people shouldn't visit others unless absolutely necessary and that only three households were allowed to mix on Christmas Day itself. A while ago we had already said we would not be able to see my aunty, uncle and cousins on Christmas day as we usually would. However, we were going to go to my mums and Kev's dad would come too.

17/12/2020 DAY 293

Back to the RVI and Vinc and Dex prior to Christmas. It could be worse could have been on it all over Christmas. Today we found out some amazing news Evie, Niamh's friend, has found a bone marrow match and will hopefully be having her transplant just after the new year. This was fantastic news, but they had been let down before, so it was a secret for now! Also, it meant a long time of not being able to see Tina and Evie as having a transplant would involve an isolation room for some time.

On our return home our lovely neighbours Mal and Karen, had set up Santa's grotto in the garden. It was a fantastic surprise and really lifted our spirits. We were able to see all of our neighbours outside and even got a visit from Santa himself!

18/12/2020 – 21/12/2020 DAYS 294-297

Niamh was excited for Christmas but still very quiet and not herself. I was supposed to go out to one of my friends for tea on Friday night, but the rules had changed again, and we were not allowed to meet indoors. Kev and I were very excited about getting Teddy and seeing the girls faces on Christmas day. We were also pleased to be able to go to my mum's and appreciated any time we got to see each other after this past year.

22/12/2020 – 23/12/2020 DAYS 298-300

Steroids finished thank goodness! We could all concentrate on looking forward to Christmas Day. Kev was working Christmas Eve, all day, so the girls decided they wanted to stay round my mums. That fit in great as we decided we would say Kev has been kept on and he would pick Teddy up and bring him back home for the night, then we wouldn't take him over to mum's until later in the afternoon after the girls had opened everything else.

24/12/2020 DAY 301

Christmas Eve. The girls and me met my aunty and cousin at the park for a little walk. We swapped presents as we would normally always be together on Christmas Day, but this year was obviously going to be very different. We then went over to Mum's house. We had booked to go to church, the COVID cases were yet again increasing, and both my mum and I didn't feel it was safe enough to go. I think this will have been the first year any of us didn't attend church at Christmas. Kev finished work and picked Teddy up, then he came over to say goodnight to the girls and returned home to have the first night with Teddy! I was to call him as soon as the girls woke up and then he would come over.

25/12/2020 DAY 302

We had the most amazing day albeit different and very quiet with just us, my mum, stepdad and Kev's dad. The girls were spoilt rotten, and Teddy was the biggest surprise ever - Niamh could not believe it!

26/12/2020 – 30/12/2020 DAYS 303-307

I was back at work for a few days, but Teddy and the girl's new presents kept them very busy! Due to people mixing more freely over Christmas and new strains of COVID the government issued more warnings and my mum decided that she felt very unsafe again especially as Kev and I were back working full time, so she went back to shielding. This was apparent at work, and we began to see the cases rising and becoming more severe than they had been previously. Niamh's consultant was still very happy with me working and being patient contact.

31/12/2020 DAY 308

Well, we were more than happy to say goodbye to 2020! Niamh and I were at RVI for a blood check and then we had arranged to have a takeaway and have an online News Year's Eve party with some of our friends from Spain. We had a great night and the girls enjoyed it.

1/1/2021 - 3/1/2021 DAYS 309-311

The start of a new year. However, things felt dismal again in relation to COVID the numbers were increasing, and a new strain was found that was making people more poorly. Niamh was on top form but the constant worry from leukaemia and COVID 19 was awful.

4/1/2021 – 31/1/2021 DAYS 312-339

Rest of the month of January was quiet and uneventful. We were back in a second lockdown and schools were again closed. With us both being back at work now we felt it was too risky to send Niamh to school for the key worker bookings, so we worked all our shifts around each other. Everyone thought school wouldn't be closed for long, again this wasn't the case. Cheer was also cancelled as were any other activities the girls did.

It was Kev's 40th but we couldn't do anything, so the girls and I made 40 cards of all the things we were going to do together when it was over. Every 2 weeks we were at the RVI -steroid weeks were still hard. Teddy was the best thing we could have done to aid Niamh's recovery; they both absolutely loved each other. He was easily trained, with just a few accidents, but we had to be strict with him as if he bit Niamh that would mean a hospital trip, which luckily never happened. Niamh had wanted a bedroom makeover for a while so we decided we would do it whilst she was off school, and we were back in lockdown.

Evie had her transplant the beginning of January and they needed to stay in an isolation ward for approximately 6-8 weeks. I thought of

Tina and all this time away from her husband and son it was very hard for them, but the positivity they showed throughout it all it was incredible. Evie would make little clips informing everyone how she was, and she actually shaved all her hair off on camera. This brought tears to my eyes as they were so inspirational it made me feel very shallow about how I felt when Niamh's hair had fallen out. However, as Tina later told me they had time to prepare for this and discuss it at length, unlike Niamh's which happened very suddenly. I sometimes felt silly I had tried to keep hold of Niamh's for so long with the little wispy bits in bunches, but hindsight is a wonderful thing and the way I felt at the time I don't think I could have cut them off!

February 2021 DAYS 340-368

We were able to get a little clip in Niamh's hair this was monumental for us!

Teddy was finally allowed out for a walk and although he was the perfect puppy in every other way he would not walk! The only place he would happily walk was on the beach. We had lots of winter seaside walks, Seaton and Saltburn being our favourite at least it got us out and gave Niamh some fresh air. Niamh kept developing the very bad chemo rash that came all over her face. We were referred to dermatology, everything that was tried was trial and error and, in the end, we found Elizabeth Arden 12 hour cream worked the best. School was still closed, and home working ensued. I was working from home, when able, but also now seeing patients face-to-face. We had quite a lot of snow and it was lovely on days off to take Niamh out sledging in her lunch hour from home schooling, she loved it and Teddy preferred sitting on the sledge rather than walking!

Niamh should have been in theatre which would have been easy to isolate prior due to her being off school, but Jagoda rang a few days before and said it was extremely busy list and they needed to cancel Niamh until 4 weeks' time. Obviously, this wasn't what we wanted to hear but we had to think that others were in greater need than Niamh and being 4 weeks away would make no difference to her. In cycle 3 maintenance now and her hair was growing lots, it was now brown and curly! I saw an advertisement for a charity walk for Clic Sergeant, the charity that support parents when their children are diagnosed. It was for 500,000 steps in the month of March, so I talked Mel and Sarah into it. Jan did it too in Fort William and Terry did his own as well.

March 2021 DAYS 369-400

One entire year since diagnosis felt a great achievement! I couldn't believe we have got this far and the difference in Niamh in a year. We were so disappointed we could not go out to celebrate but never mind we got Niamh's favourite takeaway instead and played family games. This had become our life now and it is so strange how you adapt to this new life and 2 weekly hospital visits. Evie was in hospital she had her bone marrow transplant in January she was doing well and during our hospital visits we would wave at the window as they were in complete isolation. Niamh had started some Skype singing lessons, she was loving them, and it gave her a hobby she could do, even in Covid. Finally, schools were back open just as Niamh had to isolate after her PCR test for theatre again and then they were closed for Easter Holidays - I could not believe schools were again closed this long! We had to record our steps every day and really needed about 17,000 steps a day in order to complete our target by the end of March we all did it and raised much needed funds for CLIC Sergeant. We were on the virtual audience of Ant & Decs Saturday Night Takeaway so that was a fun Saturday night in lockdown. Niamh was excited about her birthday and as lockdown was finishing, we decided to let her have three of her friends round to play in the back garden.

April 2021 DAYS 401-431

Niamh's birthday was on a school day. She was so pleased and eager to be back at school, she went without opening a single present, then came in later and opened them all when family came round. We had a little garden party for her birthday with three friends, they absolutely loved it, and it was so nice to see her playing again and some normality resuming. The weather was lovely this April and we had some great times in the garden. Niamh was really getting her strength back and loving being back at cheerleading again. We had some work done in the house and a new bathroom fitted, it was so lovely to be able to do things again that we had taken for granted prior to all of this happening.

On 17/4 Niamh had been to cheer and then come home it was a lovely day and she was in the garden playing. She went to bed ok then woke at 0100 she was feeling unwell her temp was 37.6, I had to ring the ward they told me to do her temp again in an hour. She was unsettled, I laid in bed with her, but she could not settle herself. We did temp again an hour later it was 37.5 – the ward said just to monitor her unless it went to 38. Lots of unslept hours of me worrying, temp rechecking and Niamh unwell. She was sick a few times and looked very pale, I thought it would be unlikely that she would be neutropenic, as she had just been on steroids the week before! At 5am her temp hit 38! Ward was called again, and they wanted to see her and asked if I should ring ambulance - I said no I would drive her. Working in the NHS makes you realise the demand on the ambulance service; Niamh was not unwell enough that she would need urgent treatment in the back of an ambulance, therefore it was quicker and more reasonable I would take her. As is protocol, now, we have to go to A&E at our specialist hospital first due to COVID 19. It wasn't a pretty sight at 0600 on a Sunday morning in A&E waiting area however, we were put straight into a side room, due to Niamh being at high risk of infection. She was shattered by now and just wanted to sleep on the trolley, I was very tired too and could have done with my own trolley! Luckily, Niamh's temp had now reduced she got her port in and bloods taken to check her infection markers and whether she was neutropenic. Her bloods came back that she wasn't, and her infection markers were ok, even so, she still needed reviewing by an oncologist. As it was now 0800, they decided to wait until the day consultant came in and he would see her. We waited in A&E. The consultant seen us at 10ish, and we were discharged as he said Niamh was allowed to have paracetamol for next 72 hours if she needed it to control her temperature. I confided in him I was worried that I was letting her do too much with cheer and outside playing all afternoon in the sun. He told me she should do as much as she could and definitely to get her outside if she felt like it. Niamh had on her posh Louis Vuitton pyjamas, and everyone commented on these, at least she was well dressed for her hospital trip!

30/4/21 came! One year to go until Niamh finishes treatment!! We can't wait.

May 2021 DAYS 432-463

Cycle 4 maintenance and we managed to do our first hairstyle for a while in May! Hair up in bunches!!

Niamh's bloods were consistent every 2 weeks now there wasn't much change in any of them which was good, but she was still only maintaining 50% chemo dose. The doctors just said this is what suited her body and if bloods were levelled that's all they looked for. Steroids were always still an issue and Niamh's temperament would change for the whole 5 days, she became needy and upset and sad. I had to make sure I worked my shifts out so I was off the weekend after steroids as she wanted me with her all of the time.

We were finally able to see Evie after her transplant it was on her birthday, and we went over to visit. It was amazing seeing the girls together again in an area they could play and just be kids.

20th May another magic sleep day for Niamh. As these were now only every three months she panicked about them more now, than she had in the beginning. May's weather was not as good as April's, we had lots of rain and storms! We had planned a weekend camping at the end of May, but the weather was just awful, so we cancelled, especially with Niamh just having been in theatre. The girls were still desperate to do something as we hadn't been able to do anything for so long, so Kev booked us and our friends Mel and Andrew a hotel in Blackpool. It was cheap and cheerful, but we had fun and took them out to the theme park on the Saturday. Niamh was able to go on all the rides and loved it. We also went to one of the caravans offered by the hospital at the end of May the weather was lovely again and the girls loved swimming and going to the beach.

This steroid week has been the worst yet! Niamh is so down, and it feels like I can do nothing to make her feel better. Usually I am her comfort however, this time everything I did was wrong, and she was against me all the time! It was extremely hard, but I had to tell her off a few times as she wasn't being nice to me or Issy at all and extremely demanding, speaking very rudely. I have never let my girls speak to me like this and I was not making an exception now. Of course, when she was told off it was like the worst thing ever and completely heightened by steroids. Parenting is hard, parenting on steroids is even harder as you know a lot of the behaviour is down to the medication. However, I felt rules still needed to be in place as life must carry on for these 5 days! Whether I did the right thing I will never know, and it is a constant battle with myself. It was around this time Rueben, Lacey and Niamh were all in maintenance and they all had steroids together, along with another little girl Perrie. Perrie had Acute Lymphoblastic Lymphoma – meaning it was in her lymph nodes rather than her blood. She had exactly the same treatment as the others however, just six weeks after Perrie was diagnosed, she developed a life-threatening infection which spread so quickly throughout her little body she was taken to intensive care (PICU). No doctors in the RVI had ever seen it before spread so quickly so two specialist doctors were airlifted to the RVI and saved her life. She is doing amazingly now but is still very weak due to the amount of time she spent in PICU. Her muscle mass has gone, and she uses a wheelchair, having regular physio to use crutches, and start walking again. Anyway, due to our group hatred of steroids and our five days of hell we decided to set up a steroid support group where we could chat to each other. We did joke that Geoff should have been giving us food vouchers to pay for the additional food they ate and parents gin on prescription for these 5 days every month!

June 2021 DAYS 464-494

Lovely weather again in June, meant we were able to enjoy many walks with Teddy. One of which was to a fantastic local waterfall where Issy jumped straight in. Niamh would have done the same and not given it a second thought, before this journey, now she is definitely more nervous about things and certainly not as adventurous. However, this probably has a lot to do with her port and our concerns around that too.

A big month again June as we worked out that Niamh had just ten rounds of Dex/Vinc left. As this is by far the worst part of her treatment, we encouraged Niamh to make a planner of the 5 days for the last 10 treatments and she enjoyed ticking them off. We decided she could have a treat of her choice after each steroid pulse to help her manage them better. Our steroid group definitely helped me get through these five days every month, just having someone to talk to who understood and was going through the same thing at the same time, was a tremendous support.

Niamh's school held a 'Race for Life,' as most events like this had been cancelled around the country and the school wanted to support Niamh and do something for charity and fun for the children. One of Niamh's fantastic teachers arranged it all, Mr Hill. Our local football team Middlesbrough FC brought their mascot along, Rory the Tiger, to cheer all the kids on. Unfortunately, I was the only parent allowed in to see the kids having such fun as Covid restrictions were still all in place and children had to be kept separate in 'bubbles.' It was lovely seeing all the children, who just like the 'Race for Life' had a 'back sign.' Some children had put on family members, and lots had written after the 'I RACE FOR LIFE FOR' – 'Niamh'. Some had put their expressions on 'I think she is so brave' 'she takes lots of medicines' - many of these children were not even in Niamh's year or her friends but their sentiments were outstanding. I felt very emotional and privileged to be there and witness the event.

A massive shock for us, in the beginning of June, as one of the most amazing little girls we had met at the beginning of our journey died. Lexie was the first little girl we had properly talked to on ward 4, when Niamh was diagnosed, and we were moved into the same bay. We had seen Lexie a few times since that first time on ward 4. She didn't have leukaemia but had a different type of cancer - an osteo sarcoma a type of cancer that is found in the bones. She was the most amazing little girl who had been through so much treatment, her cancer spread she had her leg amputated, sadly it continued to spread. I really didn't know what to tell Niamh, she spoke about Lexie all the time, but we didn't often see her as she wasn't there on our treatment days. Cowardly, I didn't tell her for a long time. It affected Issy also as she often went onto my Facebook and she saw a post from Lexie's mum, Suzie. I think reality hit with her a little bit about how poorly these children actually were, and she was quite upset about it despite never having met Lexie.

A massive achievement for all of us especially Niamh. Evie and her family had organised a charity bike ride around Kielder Lake to raise money for Anthony Nolan who had found Evie's bone marrow donor. Anyone who isn't registered please do - what an amazing thing you could do to save someone's life! We all rode a whopping 26.2miles around the lake!! I couldn't believe Niamh managed it, especially since I didn't think to pack any food so everyone on the ride shared with us, it was a bit like 'Jesus feeding the 5000', with 2 fishes and 5 loaves of bread!

July 2021 DAYS 495-536

1st July and hospital day for Vinc/Dex time. Before the steroids kicked in and enjoying the lovely sunny day it was Niamh and I stopped off at the Angel of the North monument on our way home. The angel had been a big part of our travelling up and down to the RVI as we always passed it and I felt in some strange way it looked out for us. Although Niamh was doing absolutely amazing, and we hadn't had a hospital stay since October not wanting to tempt fate by writing this! The ward and other parents were never far from my mind. I constantly thought of parents finding a high temperature, making an urgent dash to A&E, calming their child before an emergency access of their port, pacing the floor and listening to beeping machines all night. It was certainly something I thought about a lot and often I wished I could do more for the parents and children that were inpatients more often than us. My good friend Claire and Jojo were having a really rough time at this moment, in and out of hospital very frequently. Feeling quite helpless I tried to do what I thought I would appreciate and made Claire some nice homemade meals and bought Jojo some activities to do. It just showed how one person's journey of the same illness can be so very different from another's.

Unfortunately, COVID 19 hit a big high again in school and therefore Niamh needed to be absent the last week, prior to breaking up. She missed all the fun activities and was upset but we reasoned it was more important she was safe. She was in theatre again and it gave me time to discuss with Jagoda, that we were considering going to Spain to see my dad. It was something Kev and I had discussed at length. Kev as ever extremely overcautious was naturally very worried but even he saw the benefits for us all to go on holiday. She said we should get ourselves there, I rang and told Kev and he booked our flights however, we decided not to tell the girls just yet until we were sure Niamh's bloods were ok prior to going. We obviously needed to work the holiday around hospital appointments too, so to get the longest time we decided we would travel the day after her next appointment. She would be on steroids again, but it was a small price to pay, and we reasoned she would probably feel better away too and seeing her nanny and papa for the first time in 18 months! Jagoda also kindly swapped our appointment for two weeks later so we could get an extra day away. We told the girls two days before we were to fly – Issy wasn't happy she only had 1 day to get all her stuff packed! Niamh was so excited, she stood on the chair and jumped up and down! Holiday insurance was a big issue, one of those things you don't normally think about, now declaring all Niamh's medications and that she was still on active treatment proved to be a big cost, but sooo worth it! Steroids kicked in on the day we were flying, and I had to ask the airport to make a plate of bacon before flying!! I also made sure my dad had bacon in the fridge in Spain! It was amazing to see my dad in the airport after all this time.

August 2021 DAYS 537-568

We had the most amazing two weeks in Spain. It was exactly what we all needed. I was able to get Niamh's hair in a little ponytail for the first time and it grew so much in the sun. Just before we were leaving, she had little plaits put in at the front, and loved it. It was Issy's 15th birthday whilst we were there, and she wanted to go jet skiing. Kev took Niamh on too and they loved it.

For years, we had gone on our annual camping Bank Holiday weekend at the end of August to Pickering, with family and friends. Last year we had stayed in a cottage as we were concerned about Niamh and sharing facilities. This year we decided to go with it and go camping again. However, typically, it was the weekend Niamh was on steroids again! It was difficult to say the least. Niamh was struggling and it was hard in the tent having no reprieve. Obviously, there were so many of us we had to just go with the flow of what everyone wanted to do and sometimes it was a bit much for Niamh. Luckily Teddy was there with us, and he gave Niamh lots of cuddles. I looked forward to the following year when things wouldn't have to be arranged around steroid week!

The fun day that we tried to organise for last year was now well underway being organised for this September. COVID 19 continued to be a concern, but we were determined for it to go ahead this year.

September 2021 DAYS 569-598

Back to school for both girls, what an amazing feeling after the uncertainty of the past 18 months. Fundraising was well underway with the arranged charity funday and lots of preparation was needed prior to it going ahead. Raffle prizes, tombola set up, inflatables plus arranging everything else. The day was an amazing success everyone enjoyed themselves, the weather wasn't perfect but although we had showers lots of people turned up and we raised a whopping £7000! Making all the hard work well worthwhile.

21st September brought what we had dreaded the whole time, Issy tested positive for COVID! She was amazing and stayed in her room for a full 10 days! At this point the rules had changed, and the rest of the household were able to go out if they tested negative. Luckily, we all stayed negative and Issy was a little star again, never once complaining and keeping herself completely isolated. I informed the hospital and once again we had to be segregated when we went into the unit.

Niamh had a charity colour run organised by her school with the proceeds going towards Children's Cancer North, it was a shame again that Niamh was on steroids, but she managed a few smiles for the photos! We also had a ball to attend on the weekend Niamh was on steroids, my mum came around to babysit and had a hard time from Niamh which gave her full insight of steroid life! We joked she should have maybe joined the steroid group chat for the night!

October 2021 DAYS 599-629

Teddy was 1! Niamh blew up loads of balloons and bought him his favourite of presents a dummy! We managed to get over to Spain for another week at half term, which was lovely.

The girls were both back into school and life certainly felt normal again apart from our every 2 week's appointment.

November 2021 DAYS 630-659

We finally got round to having some of our cancelled breaks. Kev and I had a lovely night away at a hotel and I went with my mum, aunty and cousin to Edinburgh for some Christmas shopping. I also spent a night in Manchester to celebrate my friends' birthdays. At long last we had a weekend in Center Parcs which had been cancelled 3 times, as usual bad planning, Niamh was on steroids for the weekend, despite this we still had a lovely time as it was a long-awaited break. Whilst we were in Center Parcs I missed out on my friend, Nicola's 50th birthday party, she told everyone she didn't want gifts and put a jar on the side for collections towards 'Niamh's Team' very kindly raising money for Children's Cancer North. What a selfless task and very appreciated.

Niamh competed for her school in a football match and her team came 2nd out of all the schools.

December 2021 DAYS 660-690

We were unsure how we could beat last year's Christmas present, which of course was Teddy. Although, this Christmas we were able to see all our lovely family and friends and we got a surprise visit, my brother arrived from Thailand with my baby nephew Arthur, who none of us had met, apart from on facetime. This was very exciting for the girls, and they enjoyed spending lots of time with him.

We also managed to coordinate a hospital visit with Evie and had some lunch and shopping in Newcastle after the girls' check-ups were done.

Issy had her first cheer competition in nearly 2 years, and it finally felt as if the world was getting over COVID and life for us felt good.

On this journey you get a massive reality check sometimes and I heard that Billy – one of the first little boys we had met on the day unit had died on the 10th December aged just 4 years old. Remembering Billy, on the ward, the first few times Niamh was there brought a smile to my face thinking of him charging up and down the ward attached to the strongest chemo there was. He was an absolute human dynamo! Nothing fazed him in is his short life and he always had a cheeky grin on his face, you couldn't fail to feel uplifted when you were around him and admire his zest for life. When you live and breathe these clinic appointments for so long, I'm not sure if it was worse due to COVID but these friends you make on the ward and day unit become your security blanket, it made both Niamh and I happy to see a friendly face when we walked into the unit. For us to be able to chat and discuss things made us all feel better, and the lengthy appointment time go quicker. To hear that another child, who had gone through so much treatment in his little life, for it to fail was just not fair. Some say this journey is an emotional rollercoaster as within the same week on 16th December our very good friend and member of the 'steroid support group' Perrie rang the bell. I hoped and prayed it would be Niamh in just a matter of months.

We had a fantastic Christmas Day and New Year, very excited for the year ahead.

January 2022 DAYS 691-721

Excited for our new year and the finish of Niamh's treatment! Although as it got closer, I became more apprehensive and worried if we were tempting fate planning things. From day 1 Niamh had said she wanted a big party to celebrate finishing. Due to COVID it was even more important to plan this as we were only allowed the household to see her ring the bell in hospital so we were arranging a big party where everyone could see her!

Our worst fear also happened this month, Niamh contracted COVID! Chemo was stopped for 3 weeks. Niamh luckily wasn't unwell, she was amazingly well and had lots of energy but of course remained housebound. Her being off chemo was an insight of getting 'old Niamh' back and it made me even more excited for her to finish treatment. It makes you realise how much of a toll the treatment must be for her and the nasty side effects that ensue.

February 2022 DAYS 722-749

Kev and I finally celebrated his 40th from last year and my upcoming one. My mum and stepdad had the girls for a week, and we went to Jamaica! It was fantastic to have some time together but also worrying to be away from Niamh in case anything happened. In some ways again COVID helped, as Niamh was still off chemo, it was much easier for my mum as she wasn't used to giving her all her medication - yes if it had been needed, I'm sure Niamh would have kept her right like she does with Kev!

We worked the trip around all hospital visits, when Niamh wasn't on steroids or after theatre, I couldn't believe it when she got COVID. I was worried someone was trying to tell me something that I shouldn't be going. My mum said I needed to go, and she was right it did us the world of good. I felt guilty when we were there not just about Niamh but thinking of our friends too, some of which were having a really tough time on the ward. Your mind thinks of others who may just be getting a diagnosis or bad news. We had Niamh's second last theatre trip with Intratheacal Methotrexate this month and we were definitely on countdown for steroids now this being number 3 only 2 and 1 left, that last tablet of Dex would be a celebration in itself!!

March 2022 DAYS 750 - 780

2nd last ever steroids!! Things definitely seemed to be getting back to normal in relation to COVID, although I was still regularly getting phone calls from school regarding children in class getting COVID. I was reluctant to take Niamh out again. The world knew much more about it and the strains were reported weakened. It was hard but the reality of the lack of social input and missing school had to be weighed against the risk of infection. The oncology day unit informed me on my last appointment, in March, they would be allowing 2 adults on the ward from now on - it felt like someone had played a really nasty joke as soon as we were to finish treatment so was COVID guidance.

April 2022 DAYS 781-810

Our month! It was full steam ahead for organising Niamh's big 'Ring the Bell' Party as well as her having the last 5 days of steroids and last magic sleep. She will need to go back to theatre to have her portacath removed at some point. A long day for theatre, we waited around for hours before we were called. The ward had just begun allowing two adults in with every child. I can totally understand this for support, however, one parent in the room, waiting for theatre constantly spoke on facetime to someone in another country not having any respect for anyone else in the room and constantly ignoring the child that was with her - I did wonder what was the point of her being there? Also, another mum had 'Old Mcdonalds Farm' on repeat on child's iPad at full volume. She kept taking the child out for a walk but leaving the iPad on! I turned it off twice as Niamh was asleep, but she would come back, put it on and leave again! It might have been the only time I could have screamed 'bring COVID restrictions back' - and I can't believe I thought or typed that!!

I did not let this overshadow our momentous day. Niamh went to theatre we had taken in big hampers for both staff on the ward and theatre, the theatre staff had got Niamh presents which overwhelmed us and was so very kind. When coming back from theatre Kev and Issy were there to meet us, they weren't allowed on the ward until the actual ringing of the bell, but one of the nurses took pity on them and let them in about 15 minutes prior. Niamh had always said to Geoff she would cartwheel out of the ward after finishing treatment and of course she did! Not only that though one of the nurses joined her and cartwheeled out too. An apocalyptic moment for us all!

The big party went ahead without any problems it was such a fun positive night everyone loved it and Niamh certainly did. Niamh surprised me on the night by singing my favourite song 'Proud Mary' she had learned in preparation for the evening, she had kept it a secret from me and been practicing for weeks. Niamh had also said prior to the night she wanted to continue fundraising, therefore instead of presents we would do games where she raised another £1000.

Oh hello I haven't wrote in a while you might think I am a totally different person now and that I am back at school. We can catch up. Lets start here so I'm back at school now and cheer. I'm doing all my tiktok dances and just think after all the time you will hopefully get back to yourself. Your hair might not be the same but everyone says mine is lovely and I am beautiful so you will be the same.

Niamh age 8

Epilogue

So, 810 days of leukaemia and a whole host of treatment which included:

- 1460 temperature checks
- 367 days of steroids
- 60 visits to ward 14
- 18 trips to theatre (magic sleeps)
- 9 different chemotherapies taken
- 12 COVID swabs
- 4 emergency admissions

We had a wonderful 8 weeks we were on a high everything was fantastic.

However, it wasn't to last! The week before Niamh's second check-up we had just spent a few days away in London and Niamh was on top form. Then on the train home she started to vomit and had a low-grade temperature. I rang the ward, the next day, and spoke with Jagoda she said to take her in the day after for bloods. Typically, she woke up feeling fine that day, but we went to hospital and found out that all her bloods had dropped significantly. Her platelets were low her hb had dropped and she was again neutropenic. Jagoda reassured me it was all to do with whatever viral illness she had going on. However, for me it felt like history was repeating itself, especially with her platelets. We needed to be back the following week for repeat bloods and a port flush so had an agonising wait of 7 days – 168 hours to see what was happening inside her little body! On our proper check-up date, we seen Geoff who said that her bloods had clotted the week before so her platelets and hb were not accurate readings and were within normal ranges now. I felt ecstatic, never would I be so happy to hear this. Another week's worth of worry, I have a full head of greys now! I am not sure this worry will ever go away after this journey we have been on, however, looking forward and filling yourself with as much positivity as possible is the only option. Whatever happens in life we will tackle it just as we have this diagnosis and a national pandemic!

We also went to Spain on our annual summer holiday, we had another 'Ring the Bell' party (charity night) there which all of our Spanish friends were able to attend raising more money for 'Niamh's Team' as well as a memorable night.

To date 'Niamh's Team' have raised a staggering £36,000 not bad for fundraising throughout a pandemic. We endeavour to continue this support for this amazing charity who provide so much for the children going through this intensive treatment.

What have I learnt on this journey:

- Don't worry about the little things.

- Enjoy every moment as life is definitely too short.

- Always think what someone else might be going through or gone through.

- Steroids are the worst things ever!

Scars may heal, blood counts may normalise, years will pass but never again will the simple act of waking up to a normal, boring day as a healthy individual be taken for granted, nor go unappreciated.

A note from Kevin

Well, what an emotional read that was, you really do forget what a rollercoaster of a journey you go on! Hi everyone, I'm Niamh's dad (Kev) and I've been asked to add a short piece in the back of this book. Where on earth do I start? How do I talk about the worst time in my entire life?! People always say, 'Enjoy every moment because things can change in an instant'. 'You do not know what is around the corner'. These comments I had heard hundreds of times, thinking nothing will ever happen to me, up until now! Our little life was perfect and then in a heartbeat it fell apart in an instant, everything came crashing down around us and suddenly nothing else mattered in the world but our little girl Niamh. All those stupid and irrelevant things that we all get stressed about in day-to-day life didn't matter anymore. The only things going through my mind was will Niamh survive, what are her chances, and can we get through this? Every bit of my focus was now on my little girl and nothing else mattered! This was by far the worst day of my life and words cannot describe how I felt, I was numb, and I felt broken, I felt like dropping to my knees and screaming. I didn't know how to react, and I didn't know what to do. I felt so helpless! My little girl's life was now in the hands of the doctors and nurses, and I could do nothing. I knew I had to be strong not only for Niamh but for Victoria and our other daughter Issy. All I will say is please hang in there because things will get better!

If you have just started on this journey then I won't lie and to put it simply you are in for one heck of a traumatic experience, however, please remember it's a journey that is going to make your child better! The treatment is awful and seeing your child suffer and change as they inject chemotherapy into them is not easy, but Vic always reminded me and reiterated, 'This is what's making our daughter better!' Niamh's journey has certainly changed her, in fact it changed us all for the better! We have become stronger as a family, and we appreciate everything so much more. Those days out and holidays together mean so much more now and those minor marks on my car are no longer an issue!! I never thought I'd say this but it's only a car!!

To all the dads out there, there is one thing I have learnt and that is it's ok to cry! I found myself crying most days and still do on the occasion when I reminisce on what we have been through as a family. In fact, the slightest of things does set me off! I don't know why it just changed me and makes me appreciate everything so much more. Crying and speaking with close family and friends certainly helped me…so take note guys crying does help and so does talking. Secondly if your child convinces you to shave your hair off, think twice if you're thinning!! 2 years on I'm still bald with no chance of growing it back unless I spend 3k and do a Wayne Rooney!

We feel very fortunate and lucky to be where we are today, Niamh's hair has grown back slightly darker and with a natural wave and looks even more beautiful. She is so happy and content, our little girl is back how she should be and enjoying life! She is starting year 5 at school tomorrow 05/09/2022, in fact she's sorting her new pencil case out as I write this, all excited to be going into a new year with her friends.

Issy has just got fantastic results on her GCSEs, not forgetting the journey she has also been on over the past few years, thinking constantly and worrying about her little sister. Words cannot describe how proud I am of them both. (See I'm filling up even writing this!)

Casting my mind back to that first day when I got the devastating and terrible news, I never thought we would get to this point, so please take some reassurance and comfort in our journey.

We hope sharing our experience helps you in some way throughout yours.

From my family to yours we wish you all the love and luck in the world.

I would like to conclude by saying how proud I am of Victoria, she was our 'Rock' throughout all of this and without her I could not have got through it. She is an incredible woman, perfect in every way and we are so very lucky to have her in our lives!

Love Niamh's dad X

Printed in Great Britain
by Amazon